MW01230092

Merging
Jew &
Gentile
for Perfection

CHARLES & GLORIA JORIM PALLAGHY

BOOKSIDE Press

BookSide Press
877-741-8091
www.booksidepress.com
orders@booksidepress.com

CONTENTS

Our views must arise primarily from the Bible. Over the past 45 years or so we discovered that the Old and New Testaments combined, provide an answer to any question we may wish to ask, whether it concerns the true age of the earth or the timing of Christ's Second Coming.

Everything God has put in the Bible has a purpose. The Lord was very strict with Moses, reminding him to build the Tabernacle *exactly according to the blueprint I showed you on the mount. Do not deviate from it*. The same was true for the *Moedim* or the 7 appointed Feasts of the Lord as translated in English Bibles. Israel was never to forget the annual cycle of these solemn occasions during the 7-month religious/ecclesiastic calendar of the Hebrews. *Moedim* is derived from a Hebrew word meaning *"to repeat"*. The religious calendar and the 7 Feasts which dictated it were annually repeated and strongly tied to the seasonal harvests of barley, wheat and summer fruits which also have end-time implications. Moreover, to emphasize the gravity of these feasts in the life of the ancient Hebrews any male who did not attend and participate was to be cut off from Israel. Why has God been so adamant over the millennia? The brief answer is that it was for our benefit. They are richly prophetic of future events to be revealed in the last days to inform us of the timing and the imminent return of Christ. As one of the apostles asks in the New Testament, *"Knowing this to be so, examine your lifestyle and line it up with God's will for you"*.

Jewish concepts, often disregarded by western evangelists, are valuable as shadows of the true substance revealed in Christ, particularly where they are relevant to future events. Important keys to discovery are hidden in Old Testament Scripture. They are often deemed irrelevant and ignored in denominational churches.

We need to desire the intimate guidance of the Holy Spirit to know where to look in the Bible and how to dig more deeply into truths revealed in the Bible from Genesis to Revelation. Whether caught in the business of family life or at the workplace there is no excuse for disregarding regular readings from the Bible. Our hearts need to remain teachable. God expects us to allocate time for His Word.

The New Testament without the other testament will simply not do; God has deliberately concealed wondrous gems (Proverbs 25:2) which only make sense when both testaments are viewed together and from a combined Jewish (Messianic) and Gentile Christian background. Hence the title of this book.

The Bride of Christ

To grasp something about the bride of Christ, and who she is, we ought to become familiar with Old Testament keys. If we only restrict ourselves to the words spoken by Jesus on end-times in Matthew and Revelation, we will severely miss out. Four books pay particular attention to the bride of Christ, "*The Song of Songs*", "*Hebrews*", "*Ephesians*" and "*Revelation*". Ignorance of the symbolism within the 7-month religious calendar of the Jews, together with their mandatory three major Feasts of Passover, Pentecost and Tabernacles, together with ignorance of the symbolisms revealed in the Tabernacle of Moses and the Temple of Solomon, have led Bible teachers astray.

We recommend a companion book if you are interested in the formation of the bride of Christ. *End Times: According to Scripture* by Charles Pallaghy is a step-by-step walk through the structure and flow of the book of Revelation. The first section examines Revelation 2-3,

in which the apostle John points out that it deals with
'the things that are'; — the current state of the seven
churches in John's time. From chapter 4 onward, the
book transitions to describing *'the things that must be
hereafter'*; — in other words, future prophetic events
and the-end times. A major focus of his book is the
misunderstood symbolism of the 'pregnant woman'
giving birth in Revelation 12. Charles systematically
dismantles the conventional association of this figure
with Mary and the birth of Jesus. Instead, he shows
how she represents the glorified corporate bride of
Christ — redeemed humanity laboring to bring forth
spiritual offspring in the tumultuous end-times. Her
'man-child' who is caught up to heaven symbolizes
the privilege of spiritual rebirth and ascension into
heavenly places that all true believers experience.
However, contrary to rapture theories, Charles draws
parallels to the Exodus under Moses to argue that
Christians will have to endure some judgments and
tribulations along with the world before Christ's
return. Charles reminds us that it was only after the
3rd plague that God made a difference between the
Hebrews in Goshen and the Egyptians. They all had to
put up with the blood-polluted waters for seven days
during the first plague. All, including the Hebrews,

were digging pits in the sand in desperate attempts to find fresh water to no avail.

Israel will have to go through its scheduled times of trouble, though God is siding with his people. Charles recalls a touching moment in the Hollywood movie *Ben Hur* which demonstrated God's strange ways very well, even though the scene itself is fictitious. The reaction of Jesus captured the way God often deals with those he loves. We see a thirsty Ben about to collapse in a chain gang with a jesting Roman soldier offering him water only to draw the pitcher away again. Ben collapses. A compassionate Jesus revives Ben with water but the guard catches Jesus in the act. We next see an amazing piece of acting by the soldier who displays incredible facial contortions during the silent standoff between himself and Jesus. Charles would have awarded him with an Academy Award. The mystified guard draws away and raises his whip towards a refreshed Ben and the chain gang to get on their way. Though the film portrays the supernatural power of Jesus, Jesus does not intervene to set Ben free.

It occurred to Charles that it is consistent with God's ways in the Bible. The Holy Spirit comforts us momentarily when we are in trouble, sometimes even with a miracle as Charles has experienced, but then allows the distressing situation to continue. The Messianic Jewish host, Erick Stakelbeck, announced on *Watchman Newscast* that Israel will have to face 'the *Time of Jacob's Trouble*'. This phase of trouble in Israel was prophesied by Jeremiah (30:7). It is a period of great trouble just before the second coming of Jesus Christ. Stakelbeck then comforts all by saying not to worry because God is in control after all. We shall explain the prophecy briefly in Chapter 12.

Security During the Covid years

During the Covid years everybody scrambled for their masks. People were greatly concerned for Charles and his former wife, Milena, because they were close to 80 years old. We read of people restricted to ventilators in hospital suffocating horribly. Not even wives or children were allowed to visit them as they were dying. They left this world empty, shattered except for a strange person coming into their room with a helmet and 'space suit' without ever making eye contact. In our State not even their loved ones were permitted entry into hospitals. They perished alone. Imagine the wilderness their minds suffered as they laid motionless in bed: it must have been hell on earth for them. Refugees in multistorey blocks who had run out of food supplies were escorted back to their rooms by police wearing safety gear. They were prisoners in their apartments without food for days. People unwilling to be vaccinated were barred from work and shops, even from entry to Christian bookshops once the severe restrictions were somewhat lifted. Small businesses went bankrupt.

Some were aghast when they heard that Charles and his wife decided to be vaccinated after having committed their lives to the Lord in prayer. Nothing happened to them. However, their daughter Jenny, who works as a pathologist at a Melbourne hospital, verified that some had been severely affected by taking the shots without ever having had Covid. By the time Charles caught Covid the government was organized. As soon as he proved PCR positive a government doctor called him up to collect his $1100 antiviral medication free of charge. Charles lost all symptoms within three days. What word from the Lord did Charles and Milena put their faith in? It was Psalm 91:1-16.

My Refuge and My Fortress:

"*Whoever goes to the LORD for safety, whoever remains under the protection of the Almighty, can say to him, 'You are my defender and protector. You are my God; in you I trust.' He will keep you safe from all hidden dangers and from all deadly diseases. He will cover you with his wings; you will be safe in his care; his faithfulness will protect and defend you. You need not fear any dangers at night or sudden attacks during the day or the plagues that strike in the dark or the evils that kill in daylight. A thousand may fall dead beside you, ten thousand all around you, but you will not be harmed. You will look and see how the wicked are punished. You have made the LORD your defender, the Most High your protector, and so no disaster will strike you, no violence will come near your home. God will put his angels in charge of you to protect you wherever you go. They will hold you up with their hands to keep you from hurting your feet on the stones. You will trample down lions and snakes, fierce lions and poisonous snakes. God says, 'I will save those who love me and will protect those who acknowledge me as LORD. **When they call to me**, I will answer them; when they are in trouble, I will be with them. I will rescue them and honor them. I will reward them with long life; I will save them*'" (GNB).
We believe that the same assurance will apply to the

church who will have to suffer through some of the tribulations during the end times.

There is a practical analogue in the Bible. When Jerusalem was laid under siege several times and resisted the King of Babylon for a few years, Nebuchadnezzar finally responded violently in the years of evil King Zedekiah once his army entered the city. Thousands were killed while others were deported; All except for Jeremiah and his faithful servant Baruch. God had spoken to the Babylonians to locate the whereabouts of Jeremiah in the midst of chaos. The commander spoke kindly to Jeremiah and offered him a life of luxury in Babylon under his protection or to remain in Jerusalem if he so wished. Jeremiah chose to stay with the remnant in Jerusalem, so the commander gave him provisions. The remnant at first agreed to follow the commands of the Lord but then in fear, having betrayed Jeremiah and Baruch Jeremiah's faithful servant, they went down to Egypt together with the king of Israel's daughters where they perished (2 Kings Chapter 25; Jeremiah 40: 1-5). Therefore, there is only safety to those who obey the word of the Lord.

We see a parallel relevant to the perilous times we are living in, in the spiritual emptiness of the world and in many circles of Christianity.

Famine of Hearing the Word

"The days are going to come, declares the Almighty Lord, when I will send a famine throughout the land. It won't be an ordinary famine or drought. Instead, there will be a famine of hearing the words of the Lord" (Amos 8:11, GW).

> Note that the Lord declares that there will be a famine, not of the word of the Lord that is abundantly available on media or in churches, but a famine of hearing the word of the Lord – in other words, a lack of obedience to the word of the Lord.

God is a God of patterns. He repeats former seed thoughts in the Word in cycles on more elaborate and grander scales with the passing of time, such as the progressive revelation of the Temple, beginning with the Garden of Eden, then proceeding to altars of burnt offerings, then to the Tabernacle of Moses, then to Solomon's Temple and to its finale in Revelation 21:22 (MKJV), *"And I saw no temple in it, for the Lord God Almighty is its temple, even the Lamb"*.

If the reader is not familiar with the Garden of Eden as a prototype of God's temple, then consider vital clues such as the fact that the Garden of Eden had a gate facing East even as the first and second temples had their entrance always facing East, the rising of the Sun. Jesus, our Tree of life, was also in the Garden (Revelation 2:7; 22:14). Had Adam and Eve not been prevented from eating of the *Tree of Life* before the resurrection, they would have remained in their sin for all eternity. They would have always remained unredeemable as is the case with the angels who rebelled against God.

God only allowed Adam and Eve to be tempted by the *Tree of the Knowledge of Good and Evil* from which redemption was possible by the covering of a blood sacrifice. How did God do that? God provided fresh skins for them to wear (Genesis 3:21). Beware of apostate churches who refrain from mentioning the blood of Christ because they think it offensive! *"… For without the shedding of blood there is no remission for sin"* (Hebrews 9:22, MKJV).

In this book we have also drawn attention to the difference between a Jew and an Israelite in the modern State of Israel. Find out the difference. It is not merely local slang.

A Third Temple

Although crucial events will unfold in Jerusalem, the Kidron Valley and the Mount of Olives (Zechariah 14:4 and Acts 1:11), no believer in Jesus (*Yeshuah* the Messiah) ought to idolise Jerusalem, the Israel of old and any of its historical artefacts. Those in Christ, whether Jew or Gentile, ought to focus on their role as citizens in *Spiritual Jerusalem* that is from above. Abraham knew that he was just a pilgrim looking for a city with foundations, whose builder and maker was God (Hebrews 11:10). His heart was set on a spiritual city of God.

Nevertheless, Jerusalem will capture the world's attention according to a rather mysterious prophecy of Micah concerning the end times: It is possible that this will come to pass following the bride of Christ's call for the world to repent bringing only momentary peace (Chapter 6, a great harvest to come),

"But in the last days it shall come to pass, that the mountain of the house of the LORD shall be established in the top of the mountains, and it shall be exalted above the hills; and people shall flow unto it. And many nations shall come, and say, Come, and let us go up to the mountain of the LORD, and to the house of the God of Jacob; and he will teach us" (Micah 4:1-2). How this will play out and end is still to be revealed.

Construction of a third Temple in Jerusalem will become an abomination to God. Temple blueprints and the training of young Levites to perform Aaronic duties at the altar of burnt offerings indicate the intention by the Temple Society to resume blood sacrifices. A Messianic booklet printed in the USA raised no objection about the sacrificial animal pens in the proposed layout of the Third Temple! Don't be misled by the pattern in Scripture that God often works in threes. The true third temple is the **Temple of His Body**. We are the living stones that make up the Temple of His Body, Jesus Christ being the chief cornerstone (Matthew 21:42; 1 Peter 2:5). A corner stone is the rock upon which the weight of the entire building rests for stability.

Secondly, Scripture is clear that Jerusalem will become the seat of Satan (2 Thessalonians 2:1-4). *"And their bodies will lie in the street of **the great city, which spiritually is called Sodom and Egypt, where also our Lord was crucified**"* (Revelation 11:8, MKJV).

Our focus as either Gentile Christians or Messianic Jews must be on 'Spiritual Israel' and the New Jerusalem that God is establishing in our hearts, *"But you have come to Mount Zion and to the city of the living God, the heavenly Jerusalem, and to an innumerable company of angels, to the general assembly and church of the first-born who are written in Heaven, and to God the judge of all, and to the spirits of just men made perfect"* (Hebrews 12:22-23). This does not mean that we do not revere or support Israel. We intend to visit Jerusalem in the near future.

Some argue on very reasonable grounds, including biblical grounds, that the western Wall (Wailing Wall) of the Temple Mount in Jerusalem and the large area above, where the golden *Rock of the Dome* is located, are remnants of the Antonia Fortress built by Herod to protect the Second Temple. It would have been an ideal location for the stables of the Roman garrison. The apostle Paul was given cavalry escort when he was transferred from Jerusalem to a more secure prison in Ceasarea. Cavalry had to be at the ready within the walls of Jerusalem in case of unrest. Should that prove true, a Third Temple could be erected sooner than expected, further downhill towards the City of David without causing an immediate war. Some YouTube programs on the subject might be worth watching.

The Christian Walk: Sufferings and Testings

True messengers of Christ have suffered much on behalf of the kingdom of God. Jesus was tested in the wilderness before he began his ministry. Abraham had to forsake his kin and enormous riches in Ur of Chaldea when God called him, but he didn't obey completely. He took his father and his nephew Lot with him. The apostles were martyred, except for John whom Jesus particularly loved. He was exiled to the isle of Patmos where he received the revelation of Jesus Christ. When the Lord spoke to Saul (Paul) through a prophet during his road to Damascus experience, he was told that he would have to suffer much for the kingdom of God.

Before she was chosen to become the wife of Isaac, Rebekah, a 'type' of the bride of Christ, had to pass two tests of self-discipline. A type is a person or thing in the Old Testament that foreshadows a person or thing in the New Testament. Furthermore, any test in the Scripture is highlighted by the number 10. In Genesis chapter 24 we read that Abraham had sent his household steward to his uncle's village to seek a wife for his son in Nahor, Mesopotamia. He did not want a Canaanite woman to marry his son Isaac. Not knowing how to find her the steward rested at a well in Nahor with his caravan of ten camels and prayed to let it be the one who offers him a drink and to water his **ten** camels (Genesis Chapter 24). This was no simple request. It would require a miracle for his prayer to be answered.

What woman would willingly offer to water a stranger's thirsty camels who, by our reckoning, would require about 4 buckets of water each after their long journey? Moreover, she had to pass a second test involving the number 10. Her father and brother requested Abraham's steward that she not leave straight away but remain with them for another 10 days for an extended farewell. After the steward insisted that the matter was urgent Rebekah chose to leave her father's house immediately. This account, recorded in Genesis chapter 24, is an allegory of how Christ will choose his bride. Are you willing to do the same at this end of the age? We presume that the reader would be aware that Isaac was a type of Christ. A lamb was exchanged for his life by an angel on Mount Moriah where God commanded Abraham to sacrifice his son on an altar of burnt offering (Genesis 22:1-18). That was probably Abraham's worst test. He suffered mentally for three days as they journeyed to the mountain with Isaac carrying the wood for the sacrifice, but only once they came within sight of the hill where eventually the second Temple was built. Does that ring a bell? Isaac willingly submitted himself into the hands of his father. Isaac could have easily overcome his old father and escaped, in the same way that Jesus could have called down twelve legions of angels in the Garden of Gethsemane to rescue Him (Matthew 26:53), except for the fact that He said, "*Nevertheless, not my will but Yours be done*".

Charles often recounts a YouTube documentary of Kathryn Kuhlman who had a spectacular healing ministry in the USA during the 1940's. She was addressing a group of young ministers who clamoured to be given a similar ministry. "*So, you all want a ministry like mine? You don't know what you are asking. I had to suffer much*". One day Kathryn asked the Lord why she had been given this ministry as a woman, to which the Lord replied, "*Because the man for whom it was meant didn't want it*". Let us not be like that man who resisted God's call upon his life.

Many, many have followed Christ throughout history and taken up their cross, denying themselves. The Bible guarantees that anyone who steps out in faith will encounter difficulties. It is our testimony as well. However, we can take comfort. Whom the Lord calls He will also empower through the Holy Spirit. Jesus endured the cross for the joy that was set before Him (Hebrews 12:2).

There Will be a Bride With or Without Us

The provision of a corporate bride for the Son has been God's predestined plan from before the beginning of creation (John 17:24; 1 Peter 1:20; Revelation 13:8). This is why God created us in His likeness – weaklings but always redeemable because Christ was slain from before the beginning. He made no such promise to the angels! Abraham had two sons while his wife Sarah was alive, Isaac and Ishmael. Isaac was his father's only promised son. The promised one seed that was to crush the serpent's head was to come through the lineage of Eve, Isaac and Mary whose lineage was priestly. Her husband Joseph's ancestors were kings of Israel. This was fitting because the humble and obedient Son of God the Lord Jesus Christ, Yeshua Hamashiach, was elevated by the Father to be King and Priest in whom lives the fulness of the Godhead bodily, the three persons (Colossians 2:9): Three persons but one God, "*Shema Israel, YHWH 'elohenu YHWH ekhad. Hear O Israel, the Lord our God is one God*" (Deuteronomy 6:4).

When Eve was fashioned out of a rib from Adam upon whom a deep sleep had come (Genesis 2:21) it was prophetic of the bride to be brought forth from Christ in like manner, "*One of the soldiers stuck his spear into Jesus' side, and blood and water came out*" (John 19:34, CEV). Regardless of what we might think, God is going to bring about unity and perfection in a body of people before the end of time (Ephesians 4:11-13). It's up to us whether we choose to believe and participate. Its timely to be warned that the Lord is fast-tracking the world towards His Second Coming. Our opportunity to participate is dwindling by the day.

We have included simple questions and suggested exercises, whenever appropriate, to encourage our readers to mature further in Christ (Hebrews 6:1-2). This approach may transform your reading experience from being purely informational to transformational. There is no condemnation: Romans 8:1

No matter who we might be we all fall short of the glory of God. God is calling all of us forward. Who am I to respond to the high calling expressed in this book many might ask? None of us are worthy. Our own righteousness is like filthy rags. God knows our weaknesses and knows that none of us, no not one, can fulfil the calling he has for each one of us whether we might be a novice in Christ or be one of the well-known mega stars in Christianity. What qualifies each and everyone to participate in the process of perfection, is that Christ is our righteousness and that it is through his love and mercy that we are able to be processed according to the Father's will (2 Peter 1:1). All we need to do is to surrender to his voice and obey. Although time has become very short it is not too late.

Only the Lamb of God is worthy, but if we are in Him then he makes us worthy to be processed to maturity by the power of the Holy Spirit. We cannot, we must not, attempt to be perfected by the determination of our own flesh. Only the grace of the Holy Spirit can accomplish that in us. Otherwise, we shall become depressed because of failure.

In his famous first sermon to the church in the book of Acts, Chapter 2, the apostle Peter outlined four requirements of man to enter into the kingdom of God; to believe and come, to repent, to be water baptised, and to be filled with the Holy Spirit. As we explain in this book some are immediately filled with the Holy Spirit while others require to be taken through several steps which may take years as their understanding grows. Christians cannot assume that when they were born again that they were also filled with the Holy Spirit. The best proof of this in scripture is when Philip the evangelist converted many in Samaria to Christ demonstrating mighty signs and miracles. Yet the apostles in Jerusalem were concerned that the Holy Spirit had fallen upon none of them. It was not until Peter and John came to Samaria and laid hands on the redeemed that they were filled with the Holy Spirit.

Before Yeshua, Jesus, ascended to heaven from the Mount of Olives in Jerusalem he said that he would not leave us alone, but that he would send the Holy Spirit to comfort and to lead us into the whole truth (John 16:7). But as the apostle Paul said, that is only the beginning of our journey in Christ (Hebrews 6:1-2).

Charles and Gloria, 2024

CHAPTER 1

Our Present State of Chaos

The prophecies of Jesus concerning events before the Second Coming are coming to pass before our very eyes: "*Upon the Earth great distress of nations, with perplexity; the sea and the waves roaring. Men's hearts failing them for fear*" (Luke 25:25–26, KJV).

The year 2024 created havoc in the Asia-Pacific region, and even beyond to the Ukraine and the Hamas-Israeli wars that are draining Australian and US military and economic resources. Worldwide extreme weather events, the rise in greenhouse gases, tsunamis, melting of the North Pole and the scale of deforestation in the Amazon, to name a few, are alarming. Massive earthquakes in Japan are headlines. Locally, unruly pro-Palestinian protests are rife in Australian capital cities. North Queensland was battered with a 'one in a hundred years' flood. Thunderstorm cells are eroding the land and roadways all the way south on the 2000 km East coast, while early forest fires are gutting the drier regions this summer. Australia already had suffered enough of droughts and devastating bush fires over the last few years, not counting the executive severity in which Covid was handled especially in the State of Victoria, forcing many businesses into liquidation. Who would have ever believed that cars will be washed down the streets in Dubai?

The hypocrisy in government circles is starkly evident. My friend's multimillion-dollar company *Jim's Mowing* was prevented from servicing landscaping needs in the private sector, while in the same state council gardeners were allowed to work. Government corruption is evident. The Labour government in Victoria scrapped a tunnel project to link the prosperous eastern suburbs to Melbourne airport. The cancellation fee of 1.2 billion dollars would have paid for the tunnel: all because of a minority electorate group favourable to the Labour State Government.

Analysts openly declare that WWIII is already under way—not in open military conflict such as was the case in the two world wars, but it has already begun in the shape of economics and technology. Taiwan is alarmed by the rate at which their submarine cables are being cut, an effort presumably by the Chinese to bring them to their knees to cut them off from the outside world. Iran-backed gunboats are pirating shipping in the Gulf stopped only by US Seahawks helicopters. China and North Korea are threatening Australia, which has resolved to purchase twelve nuclear-driven submarines from the US under the AUKUS treaty. China is loaning huge amounts of money to small

Pacific nations—loans which they will never be able to repay. And it can be only called a stupid move, but the Australian northern Territory secretly leased the Port of Darwin to the Chinese for 99 years. It was too late for an angry Federal Government to intervene. The huge Chinese company Huawei was contracted to build our large installations of solar panels and introduced their mobile phones, enabling China to easily spy on Australia. Australia could be facing a total shutdown if the Chinese decide to do so. Fortunately, Australia refused Huawei to install our 5G network. All these appear to be the beginning of sorrows before the end of time as Jesus prophesied.

Much more important, of course, is that numerous prophecies concerning Israel, Jerusalem, and the Gentiles before the end of time are being fulfilled before our very eyes. There can be no doubt that the beginning of sorrows has come upon us.

"*When you shall hear of wars and rumors of wars, do not be troubled. For it must happen, but the end shall not be yet. For nation shall rise against nation, and kingdom against kingdom. And there shall be earthquakes in different places, and there shall be famines and troubles. These things are the beginnings of sorrows. But take heed to yourselves. For they shall deliver you up to sanhedrins, and in the synagogues you shall be beaten. And you shall be brought before rulers and kings for My sake, for a testimony against them. And the gospel must first be proclaimed to all nations. But whenever they lead you away and deliver you up, take no thought beforehand what you should speak or think. But speak whatever shall be given to you in that hour. For it is not you who speaks, but the Holy Spirit. A brother will betray a brother to death, and a father his son. And children will rise up against their parents and will cause them to be put to death. You will be hated by all for My name's sake, but he enduring to the end, that one will be kept safe"*, (Mark 13:8-13, MKJV). That's grim and reassuring at the same time!

Creation Groans for the Revealing of the Sons of God

"For all nature is expectantly waiting for the unveiling of the sons of God", (Romans 8:19, Williams).

The Williams translation is not alone in attributing to the word creation 'all of creation', including all material things. In Romans 20:1, the same word in

Greek (*ktisis*) is used for all of nature, including all living things.

This comes strange to western ears. Having grown up in 'western churches', I have always assumed this to be poetic use of the Hebrew used in scripture, e.g., of lions roaring for their food to God and trees clapping their hands.

Having recently married Gloria, an ex-Senior AOG pastor's wife from Port Moresby in Papua New Guinea, I was corrected not to take this as poetic writing but as it is, literal to a degree. There is some intrinsic property of things created by the spoken word of God that allows them not only to be intimately related to their creator but also respond to persons in whom the Holy Spirit dwells, such as water permitting Jesus to walk on its surface or an axe head to float to the surface so that it can be retrieved by the prophet (2 Kings 6:5-7). Obedient children of the Father have this privilege.

You may ask the question why all of creation should be crying out to God for the restoration of the sons (and daughters) of God. We need not look far for the answer. The worldwide cruelty to animals and the raping of the environment for centuries by greedy industrialists are cause enough. Deforestation is occurring at alarming rates. Certain regions in Asia cage bears and other creatures under the cruellest conditions for the extraction of highly valuable glandular secretions for medical purposes. Monkeys have been forced to inhale intense smoke by tobacco companies all their lives to examine its harmful nature and the organs it targets.

My father, an industrial chemist, wanted to examine the effects of nicotine in Hungary before WWII by placing a tiny drop of nicotine extracted from cigarette butts onto the tip of a dog's tongue. The dog died. Tobacco companies deny responsibility for health issues caused by smoking. The famous Wild West rodeos practised in many countries work on the principle of strapping the testicles of bulls and horses in such a way that when a rider mounts, it creates so much pain that the unfortunate animal will not stop bucking until it ejects its rider. Any male enjoying rodeos should know what that would mean if their own testicles were strapped and their partner should suddenly tug the strap!

True children of God would never allow any of these horrors if they ruled the planet with Christ. Mankind will once again care for the planet as did Adam and Eve before they fell into sin. The Millennium, a thousand-year rest, shall immediately follow the Second Coming of Christ and our resurrection. We shall have a new beginning where there shall be no more tears or sorrows. After the thousand years the Lord will create a new heaven and a new earth where we shall be with Him and the Father for all eternity. To gain an understanding why the Millennium is specified by God to be a period of 1000 years we recommend the book by Charles, *End Times: According to Scripture*. The book explains some of the symbolisms used in the book of Revelation and the time chart of world history, and much more.

Question 1

- How do you react when you see the car in front throw rubbish out the window?
- Examine why you feel the way you do about it.
- How does your response line up with the content of this chapter?

Question 2

- When you come across a shallow body of water have you ever been tempted to walk on water as Jesus did?
- You expected to fail, didn't you? Make a list of reasons why you knew in your heart that God wouldn't answer your desire.
- Then consider Matthew 17:20 and consider its context.
- What conclusions can you come to?

CHAPTER 2

Ancient Israel Exiled from the Promised Land

God cares about the welfare of the Earth and its animals almost as much as He cares for its inhabitants. In the Bible there is a close link between peoples and the lands they occupy. As mankind continues to ravage the land, the Earth shall react violently with earthquakes, extreme weather, and unproductivity. Mankind, false religions, and false shepherds have corrupted the Earth for millennia, and God shall see to it that the Earth shall respond correspondingly. We can read how violent those days shall be in the book of Revelation when the Earth and God have had enough. Enough is enough, God will say. God declared to the children of Israel in the times of Moses, "*You shall keep all My statutes and all my judgements, and do them, **so that the land where I bring you to live shall not spit you out***" (Leviticus 20:22). "*And you shall be holy to Me. For I Jehova* [the Lord in Hebrew, Yahweh — JHVH] *am holy, and have severed you from the nations, so that you should be Mine*" (Leviticus 20:26, MKJV).

Israel polluted the temple and the Promised Land frequently. On each occasion God brought disasters upon them, enemies to plunder their crops, diseases, and even eviction from their lands time and time again. When they offered blood on their altars, God only

11

laughed at them with derision (Proverbs 1:23–33).
Even today, people may claim salvation under the
blood of Jesus, but if they wilfully disobey the word
of God, they will reap what they have sown — God
is not mocked (Galatians 6:7).

Background: Israel Splits – Greed of Kings and People

The split was caused by the excessive greed of King
Solomon's son, Rehoboam. Israel was only united as
a nation for 120 years, 40 years each under the kings
Saul, David and Solomon. Those were its glorious years
of prosperity. Each of the two kingdoms subsequently
angered the Lord which precipitated their exile
into foreign lands. First, the northern kingdom for
worshipping golden calves and then, about 135 years

later, the southern kingdom for failing to obey how to look after the agricultural lands God had given them.

The northern kingdom which included ten of the twelve tribes were scattered worldwide by the Assyrians — the so-called 'Lost Tribes'. The southern kingdom centred in Jerusalem and comprised of Judah, Benjamin, and the corrupted Levitical tribe that serviced the Temple, was also evicted from the land. These three tribes were sent into captivity to serve the kings of Babylon for 70 years. They had not only rejected the prophets and Jeremiah in particular, but even went so far as to imprison and torture God's messengers (Hebrews 11:36-38).

God eventually reacted so violently that the sons of the King of Jerusalem, Zedekiah, were butchered before their father was blinded and put in chains in Babylon. Why? Because when Baruch brought letters of warnings from

Jeremiah, evil king Zedekiah tore them up and burnt them on the log fire while relaxing in his winter palace.

God ensured that the corrupt priests of Jerusalem, who had mocked Jeremiah, were killed. Only the very poor and Jeremiah, together with his faithful servant Baruch, were spared by the king of Babylon. They were allowed to remain in the land by God as a reward for their faithfulness in the midst of a wicked nation. What made the land vomit Israel out of the Promised Land they once possessed?

Before Judah was sent into exile to Babylon, the northern kingdom, comprised of the ten tribes, was dispersed into the Gentile world under the Assyrians who replaced their lands, mainly in Samaria, with Gentiles from the region. They were assimilated throughout the Gentile world after a few hundred years of attempts on their part to maintain their Hebrew origin and culture. These remnant cultures and social behaviours including food preferences help to identify members of the lost tribes today. Following their exile, they colonised foreign lands and cities such as Samarkand, named after Samaria. Evidence of Hebrews having been there a long time ago can be found hidden deep in the cellars of Islamic museums which don't want to admit that Hebrews once lived there before Islam. There is a steady trickle of the diaspora returning home once they discover their true origins from countries as far apart as central Asia to Morocco.

It is amazing that the apostle James included the ten tribes of the diaspora in his opening greeting when he didn't even know where they were located. God obviously meant his book to reach the ears of those returning to Israel in the latter days before the Second Coming: *"James, a bondservant of God and of the Lord Jesus Christ, to the twelve tribes who are dispersed abroad: Greetings. Consider it all joy, my brethren, when you encounter various trials"* (James 1:1–2, NASB).

Thousands of Jews have become believers both in Israel and overseas in recent years. Messianic congregations are zealously witnessing to the Jewish world winning many to *Yeshua*, the Lord Jesus Christ. They have been so successful in Israel that orthodox Jews on occasions, especially their chief rabbis, have violently campaigned against the Messianic churches. In synagogues, messianic prophecies such as found in Isaiah 53 are avoided because they clearly point to Christ. Psalm 110:1 indicates at least two persons in the Godhead, "*The Lord said to my Lord*", while in the creation account the word used for God, *Elohim*, is plural. In talking about Himself, Jesus referred to Psalm 110:1 in Matthew 22:44.

However, as scripture confirms, whatever Satan means for evil, God will turn into good but only for those who love Him (Genesis 50:15–21; Romans 8:28). It is a principle in the Word that the way to God and to abundant life is through much suffering as exemplified by Jesus Himself (Colossians 2:13–15; Hebrews 2:14–15).

Why Judah Went into the Babylonian Captivity for 70 Years

God decreed that the southern kingdom be punished for not caring for their cultivated lands in accordance with God's laws. Greed seems to have been a factor once again. We therefore need to appreciate some of the Mosaic laws regarding the care of the land and its domestic animals.

Most Christians have never heard this preached in church. Moses did not just bring the Ten

Commandments. Each of the ten commandments had to be elaborated under a large set of sub-commands as well as rules regarding service in the temple which the temple priests understood. Over time they disregarded the laws concerning the land from approximately the time of King David onwards. David was a beloved king, but he did not ensure that Israel and its Levites followed the laws of God completely even though David was filled with the Holy Spirit from time to time. To this day some Holy Spirit–filled people clearly walk in disobedience, no matter what great preachers some of them might be! What law did united Israel, begin to disobey for 490 years beginning roughly at the time of King David?

But surely David was a man after God's heart we might ask (1 Kings 11:4; Acts 13:22)?

"But to this man will I look, to the afflicted and contrite spirit, and the one who trembles at My word" (Isaiah 66:2, MKJV). *"The person I value is not proud. He is sorry for the wrong things he has done. He has great respect for what I say"* (NirV). David ably fitted those requirements.

So, how could Israel have possibly sinned during David's rule? Although David sinned personally concerning his affair with Bathsheba, and connived to see her husband murdered, how could he have led Israel as a nation astray seeing that God commended him twice in the Old Testament? (1 Kings 11:4; 1 Samuel 13:16). The answer is quite simple.

We are all familiar with the ten commandments which the Lord gave to Moses on Mount Horeb in Arabia. But that was only an overall generalisation of what God expected of the Hebrews under the Mosaic laws. To put this in context, how familiar are we with the 613 laws that not only came out of the ten commandments but also out of the daily life of ancient Israel once the Levitical priesthood was established? How many are familiar with the laws concerning a woman suspected of adultery? How were they to be tested before the Lord? Can you the reader specify what those laws were, right now, without asking Dr. Google? Have you ever even heard of them? They are in the Bible, in the book of Leviticus and elsewhere. Israel had to follow them. We just never bother to investigate obscure laws.

Likewise in the days of David. Obscure and inconvenient laws were put aside, many probably from the time of the Judges but maintaining the laws concerning the Sabbath and the religious cycles of the Sabbatical Year were of great concern to God as was the Year of Jubilee. Jeremiah was able to precisely number the years of neglect in prophesying that Israel would be placed into exile for one year for every Sabbatical year (every seventh year) they ignored.

Sabbatical Years of Rest for the Land were Ignored

One of the annually awaited benefits of Israel was the Day of Atonement, Yom Kippur, on the 10th day of the Feast of Tabernacles in the 7th month. On this holy day the High Priest had to go through the vail into the Most Holy Place and sprinkle the blood of a lamb 7 times onto the golden Mercy Seat between the cherubim on top of the Ark of the Covenant. What was its purpose? To forgive the whole nation its known sins of disobedience and, wait for it, its sins of ignorance. A sin of ignorance is sinning against a law of God one may not be aware of that it exists. Such was the state of the nation of Israel in the time of the kings.

There were laws that some of the teachers of the law obviously knew about from ancient scrolls but either overlooked them or thought them no longer relevant.

Nevertheless, God held Israel accountable for one notable law in dealing with cultivated lands every 7th year; the Sabbatical Year (Leviticus 25:1-34; Jeremiah 25:8-12). The Sabbatical Year was holy to the Lord. In fact, one should give special attention to the 7th of anything in Scripture because they are relevant to end-times even as the 7 components of the three main Feasts are prophetic of the end-times (*"End Times: According to Scripture"*, Charles Pallaghy, 2023. Bookside Press, Toronto, in colour, high resolution and A4 format).

The feasts of Passover, Pentecost and Tabernacles are known as the God-appointed times. Apart from their spiritual significance their long-term purpose was also to provide us with clues today for the timing of the Second Coming of Christ. Nowadays, Messianic Jews are delving into their deeper meanings with some degree of success. God will reveal more and more to devout followers of Christ as the time of his return approaches ever closer. We all need to know what's ahead or the book of Revelation would have never been written. Revelation is not all doom and gloom. It deals with the progressive formation of the bride of Christ and her mission to the world.

Regarding the care of the land under the Mosaic laws Charles once asked a Hebrew friend about the Sabbatical Year during his visit to his home in Rehovoth, Israel. All this man's personal books were in the Hebrew tongue. Charles' friend was a Zionist who was proud that his forefathers had been born in Jerusalem. He inherited and very successfully managed valuable orchards in the valley below the Golan Heights, "*Have you ever rested your orchard in the 7th year?*", Charles asked, to which he replied, "*What do you mean?*" Charles reminded him about Leviticus chapter 25. "*Oh, no!*" he said quickly, "*I would lose too much money if I did that*". He made great profits by sending ripe fruits to the European Markets before other growers could. Perhaps there was something of that attitude too in the hearts of the early Israelites which made them forget Leviticus 25:2-7 (MKJV),

"*Speak to the sons of Israel and say to them, when you come into the land which I give you, then shall the land keep a sabbath to Jehovah. You shall sow your field six years, and you shall prune your vineyard six years, and gather in the fruit of it. But in the seventh year shall be a sabbath of rest to the land, a sabbath for Jehovah. You shall neither sow your field, nor prune your vineyard. You shall not reap that which grows of its own accord of your harvest, neither gather the grapes of your undressed vine. It is a year of rest to the land. And the sabbath of the land shall be food for you, for you and for your servant, and for your slave woman and for your hired servant, and for your stranger who stays with you. and for your cattle, and for the beast that is in your land, shall all the increase of it be for food".*

Later in the Chapter the Lord described what he was going to do during the Year of Jubilee. The Year of Jubilee is scheduled for the year that follows the 7th Sabbatical Year. God ended his instructions with the warning, *"You shall fear your God. For I am Jehovah your God".*

These verses make it clear that God commanded them to rest the land from its labour every 7th year (the Sabbatical Year). However, they did not respect the 7th year of rest for the land over a period of 490 years, 70 cycles of 7 years. Therefore, God sent the southern kingdom into exile to Babylon for 70 years, one year for every Sabbatical Year missed.

The Sabbatical Year was very special in other ways too. Debts were forgiven and Hebrews who had sold themselves into slavery to their fellow men to pay off debts were released and allowed to return to their families. The Year of Jubilee was even more special. After every 7x7 (49) years, in the Year of Jubilee, property had to be returned to their original Hebrew owners as well thus maintaining the tribal and family ownerships of their lands over millennia. Of importance in understanding prophecy, is that this privilege was not extended to Gentile slaves.

The Number 7

As we have already seen God loves the number 7. The Father has planned the creation, world history and the religious calendar of the Hebrews in cycles and patterns of 7's. God worked for 6 days and then rested on the 7th which we call the Week of Creation. To remind the nation, God has called mankind to work for 6 days and to rest on the 7th day which was the norm a hundred years ago and earlier. God considers the 7th day most holy, the Sabbath. Sunday, the 8th day, was a new beginning for the following week. Anyone found working on the Sabbath was to be put to death on the Lord's orders, even if he was only found collecting sticks. Out of interest, the number 8 is Bible code for a new beginning. Watch out for it when reading the Bible. How many people on the Ark had a new beginning in the days of Noah?

Australian universities follow the British and US systems of 'resting' their academic staff every 7th year. When Charles was first appointed as a university lecturer (professor in USA) in 1971 his contract included a paid sabbatical year for every 7th year of tenure. The intention is to give academic staff one year in seven to carry out honorary research work or study at any institution around the world. This period of rest from normal hectic activity gave staff a fresh insight into their research and develop a useful network of colleagues overseas.

The West adopted this system from Israel. At the time of the Israelites' slavery under the Pharaohs in Egypt (symbolic of the world's systems) Yahweh God inaugurated a new beginning in the Hebrew calendar. He placed within the complex civil 12/13 months lunar calendar of the Hebrews the annual religious or ecclesiastical calendar, exactly six months out of phase with the civil calendar. He called it a new beginning. It was the beginning of the 8th month. Through the mouth of Moses and his brother Aaron, the Lord placed great significance on the first seven months of the religious calendar. Nisan is the first month that brings honour to the Lord for all of time (Easter or Passover, Exodus Chapter 12). The seventh month of the civil calendar, Tishri, was nominated as the first month, Nisan, of the ecclesiastical year. The Hebrews refer to Nisan as *chodesh-ha-yeshua*, meaning the month of salvation in English. God elaborated on the three major Feasts which were designed to begin and end in the first 7 months.

Charles discovered that God utilises the number seven, or seven of anything throughout the Bible, as a signpost that the immediate context or principle of the subject matter mentioned is relevant to end-times. For example, in the book of Esther, how many handmaidens were allotted to Esther and how many wise counsellors did King Ahasuerus have? The rejection of Vashti, the haughty queen, and the rise of humble Esther in the King's eyes reflects the rejection by King Jesus of the false queen,

Christian denominations ruled by the spirit of Babylon (Revelation 18:7), and the choice of His heart, the genuine bride of Christ.

Return of the Exiles to the State of Israel

As we have already seen, Leviticus chapter 25 stresses that the land, the earth, and the animals living on it should also have their seventh year of rest. Because Israel disobeyed, Israel was punished severely; it was not merely discipline. Many perished. *"And the ones who had escaped from the sword he carried away to Babylon, where they were servants to him and his sons until the reign of the kingdom of Persia, to fulfill the Word of Jehovah in the mouth of Jeremiah, until the land had enjoyed its sabbaths. All the days of the desolation it kept the sabbath, to the full measure of* seventy years" (2 Chronicles 36:20–21, MKJV). God's recompense was ruthless. As scripture states, *"Behold then the kindness, and the severity of God; on those having fallen, severity; but on you, kindness, if you continue in the kindness. Otherwise, you also will be cut off"* (Romans 11:2, MKJV).

We can safely surmise from scripture that, because the State of Israel has placed a high priority on turning its deserts into fruitful fields since its inception in 1948,

God's favor and focus is returning to Israel and to the ten tribes dispersed among the Gentiles. It's been a hard road since 1948 and it still is.

Israel exercises a policy to take good care of its environment and animals even as God desired in the beginning, "*Let us make man in our image, after our likeness: and let them have dominion over the fish of the sea, and over the fowl of the air, and over the cattle, and over all the earth, and over every creeping thing that creeps upon the earth*" (Genesis 1:26, ESV, also 1:27–30). *"And the Lord God took the man and put him in the garden of Eden to tend and guard and keep it"* (Genesis 2.15, AMPC).

Israel will play a central role during end-times, but not by excluding Gentile Christianity as seems to be the subconscious mindset amongst a few Messianic Jews. Subtle hints of nepotism have come to the attention of Charles when he views Messianic programs coming out of Israel. God intends to bring forth a glorious bride of Christ comprised of both Jew and Gentile.

God will have his way on the Earth even before He creates a perfect New Heaven and Earth (Isaiah 65:17–22; 2 Peter 3:13; Revelation 21:1–7). Not to miss out, the Earth will have its thousand-year rest in the presence of Christ and all the resurrected faithful, during the 7th Day of the Redemptive Week (2 Peter 3:8) as shown in the time chart in Chapter 10.

Question 1.
- If you live in an affluent society and have a well-paying job, do you take its benefits for granted?
- If you are living in poverty, how do you feel about your circumstances?
- In either case, make a list of reasons why you feel the way you do?
- Where would you look for answers in your situation?
- How would a drastic change in your circumstances affect you?

Question 2.
- What is your attitude to the amount of time you are spending on earning your living?
- What determines whether you attend a church or not?
- Do you feel that you should be spending more time considering your eternal future?
- What kind of things distract you from spending more time in the Word of God?
- List in each case the reason why.

Question 3.

- Why do you think the chart in Chapter 10 is referred to by Bible students as the "Redemptive Week"?

- How long did Adam and Eve live in the Garden of Eden before they sinned? Read the first five chapters of the book of Genesis for the answer.

- How long could Adam and Eve have lived if they hadn't eaten of the 'Tree of Knowledge of Good and Evil'?

- Considering the seven days of creation can you pin-point the time when Adam and Eve sinned by eating of the forbidden fruit? If not, why not? If possible, refer to what Charles wrote about it in his book, *End Times: According to Scripture*.

CHAPTER 3

Astounding Privileges Through the Blood

A friend of Charles, Val, was walking along the beach with her husband at a remote location where they camped. After a while, her husband decided to return to the camp site, but she continued to walk along the beach. A few hundred yards further on, she noted two dogs coming out from the amongst the sand dunes to play in the waves. One of them turned his head and fixed his eyes on her. She became afraid. A few surfers were way out to sea, much too far to call them for help. She had just seen on YouTube a video of a bull terrier in the UK who had attacked a lady. Although the police shot the dog several times, it died with her wrist still in the grip of his teeth. The jaw had to be forced open to release her hand for treatment. Many domestic dogs of this breed have had to be put down in Australia for the same reason.

The dog began to approach her with fierce determination. When it came within six yards, she held out her hand and twice commanded it to stop in the name of Jesus. It stopped dead in its tracks, turned around, and slunk back to the other dog and walked back into the bush.

We see many examples of the power of God's people over nature, especially in the Old Testament. A classic example is that of Elijah who called down fire each time a troop had been sent out to arrest him. The third group fell on their knees before Elijah and begged him saying that they are only following their master's command and have no intention of harming him (2 Kings 1:9–15). Children mocked Elisha the prophet because he was bald. Elisha cursed them whereupon two she bears came from the woods and killed 42 of them (2 Kings 2:23-24).

Western Christianity is generally ignorant of the power God has given over nature to those who abide in Him (John 14:12). When we exercise power, it's not because the created object or living thing has a mind that can respond, but apparently because of an intrinsic link to the spoken word from God which created it (Hebrews 1:3–6), whether it be a pen, a car, or a plant—all these are present because of an initial creative Word. Anything that exists, exists because of God who brought it into being from raw materials that He spoke into existence. Mankind's role has been to modify it! This is why God can claim that "*all things are mine*" (Psalm 24:1; Ezekiel 18:4).

When we speak by the anointing of the Holy Spirit, according to the will of God, it modifies the created object to behave accordingly. It is not something we can play with to suit our whims. Praising nature which pleased God when He first created (Genesis 1:31) allows us to receive a blessing through the thing created. If we curse every rock we stumble on, then nature will respond accordingly, and we receive the recompense from a cursed creation (Genesis 3:17)— strange but true as Gloria has experienced in her life.

When we praise the creation, we are obeying the mandate God has given man to rule over the creation (Gen. 1:26)—in godly fashion, like a productive gardener who cares for his crop and environment. We therefore should not be surprised when the Lord blesses such a person who gives thanks to God for a good harvest or gives thanks over a meal as Jesus always did! (Luke 24:30).

I saw on YouTube the following testimony. Some years ago, a contingent of Russian farmers visited Israel to learn of their renowned ability to turn deserts into fertile land. The visitors asked, "*How many kilos of potatoes do you get per.....?*" The Israeli agronomists quickly responded, "*Let's not talk about kilos but tonnes.*" They raised their conversation by a factor of 1,000. It's like a small-time banker talking about thousands of dollars to New York investors, while the New Yorkers would be likely to respond, "*Stop trifling. Let's talk about millions.*"

"*And God said, let us make man in our image, after our likeness: Let them have dominion over the fish of the sea, and over the fowl of the air, and over the cattle, and over all the earth, and over every creeping thing that creeps upon the earth*" (Genesis 1:26, ESV).

We often ask the Father for far too little because of our lack of faith! God has more for us, much more if we are patient enough. He has infinite resources by just speaking a word. Nothing is too hard for God.

Gloria and Charles are confident that kind words spoken by marriage partners into their marriage situation can restore broken marriages. The spoken word is powerful and creative!

We are not promoting the prosperity gospel preached by some where people attempt to force God into rewarding them in return for something that they may have done in the name of the Lord. Of course, if we don't abide in Him, we can ask but will not receive. God does not respond to demands.

Catherine Marshall, in her wonderful 1955 book and movie 'A Man Called Peter', discovered that lesson after she had been lying in bed for many months with TB. She and her husband, who led prayers in the Senate, were frustrated because they could hardly meet their needs in their manse in Washington DC especially with her in bed like an invalid. She had always demanded healing according to the scriptures, but the moment she surrendered her expectations to our loving Father, she was instantly healed. God told him during his sermon about Catherine's healing. He rushed home to find her coming down the staircase, a very touching moment in the film.

Question

- Do you feel that you have no right to speak a word of command to the creation, even in desperate situations?
- List your reasons separating them into three categories: Never knew I could; Experiential; Scriptural.
- Elaborate on each. What do they tell you about yourself?

CHAPTER 4

Practical Reality of Genesis 1:26

Testimony of Charles

Gloria is unusually devoted to God. One of the reasons Gloria became attracted to me over the internet, before we met face to face in Australia in 2023, is that I mentioned to her one day that I have some Jewish Ashkenazi DNA from my father's side of the family. In some PNG provinces the people hold Jews, and anything associated with Jews, in very high regard for no better reason than because God seems to will it so. Papua New Guinea has opened a full embassy in West Jerusalem which Israel is willing to fund for the first two years. That is amazing for a small Pacific nation. Many Papua New Guineans are willing to spend huge amounts of money to visit Israel which astounds me. Is there a spiritual reason behind it, I wonder??

The Jewish Ashkenazi communities in central Europe such as in Germany, Hungary, Poland, and in Russia have a characteristic DNA fingerprint. Our relationship blossomed when Gloria revealed that years earlier, she took her teenage children at great expense to visit Israel. They planted three olive trees in a special reserve in Jerusalem.

I was greatly surprised when I first read the report on my DNA analysis. Growing up in Australia but having gone through bombing raids and machine gun fire in Hungary and Germany, I admired German weaponry in my youth. Fortunately, I had not been old enough to join the Hitler Youth, but I used to love their stirring marching songs about the alps and the Fatherland. At the same time, long before I became a Christian, I took a liking to some Jews and anything to do with barren wastes such as the Sahara. I love the film '*Lawrence of Arabia*" with Peter O'Toole. The music accompanying desert scenes has a mysterious hypnotic effect on me as did the brief scene with Jesus offering water to a thirsty Ben in the Hollywood epic '*Ben Hur*'. It somehow ties me to the barren landscapes in Israel.

My older sister recalls that during the war the husband of our neighbour in Germany would come home sobbing every day. Nobody knew why. His distraught wife used to invite my mother over for comfort during the day. I suspected that he had been a worker in a concentration camp. Sure enough, Ohrdruf was nearby when I looked at a map once I became a Christian. General Eisenhower was disgusted by what he saw after they liberated Ohrdruf. He ordered the German locals to carry all the wasted bodies out. I hasten to add that there were many Germans who helped the Jews one way or another. They were generally discovered and incarcerated. *'Abgeschleppt'*, literally meaning *'to have been dragged away'*, is a word that still rings in my ears 80 years later. It is very descriptive of what the Gestapo dressed in civies did with their car waiting outside. My maternal grandfather, a Lutheran Pastor in Germany where we lived through the end of the war, hated Hitler.

My mother recalled her father risking arrest by only offering a very limp *"Sieg Heil"* salute to greet members of his congregation on the  street. The photo is that of Pastor Friedrich Oels and my auntie Inge (in plats). Pastor Oels would take me through snow laden forest tracks in the hills while bombers droned away overhead. We loved collecting the aluminium streamers the Americans dropped to fool German radar. They looked lovely at night on our Christmas tree gleaming in candlelight with us singing '*Silent Night*'. Once he yelled out to prevent me from picking up a booby-trapped toy tank dropped by one of the allies. I imagine he prayed a lot for us.

This photo shows me and my sister Elizabeth with our mother when I was close to three years old (taken in Hungary before we fled to Germany from the advancing Russian front). I had the appearance of a typical Aryan. A distraught Polish nun, whose village had been ravaged by the German army, was stopped in the nick of time by a Hungarian doctor when he caught her trying to give me a lethal injection in hospital. I was called the 'little Hitler' because I always conversed in German with my mother (*Mutti*) in the Hungarian hospital.

I am somewhat proud that I have some Jewish heritage. I showed a photo of my Hungarian father, with his twin brother (smoking) and a friend (glasses), playing cards with my grandmother. Everybody commented that she looked a typical Jewess, although she was a Catholic when she married my Hungarian protestant grandfather. According to my DNA the family apparently gained Jewish blood five generations earlier. My father had a pronounced hooked nose. I used to ask him in Australia, *"How come Hitler never had you arrested?"* He never answered and never wanted to talk about the war or the chemical factory IG Farben where he was an industrial chemist. In Hungary he had been director of a magnesium plant. My father was grieved whenever I wanted to know something about the war from an adult perspective. He hated the war and threatened to destroy our TV set if I watched another war film involving Germans. He used to disappear to northern Germany from Thuringia where we lived for 2 years with my German grandfather at the Lutheran manse. My father rarely came home from work except on God-ordained occasions when he would save us from getting killed.

No wonder that he hated remembering those years. According to a map I consulted, railway tracks from Bergen Belsen concentration camp passed by the factory. Did the prisoners ever get safety gear? I suspect not. I still remember the sting at Melbourne University when I picked up an old bottle of fuming hydrochloric acid without wearing gloves. Fortunately, there was a tap nearby. The holocaust was a tragedy. When I became an adult, I heard that as inmates were being marched off to the gas chambers the occasional rabbi would yell out, "*There is no God*". More comprehensive information on Charles can be found at www.creation6000.com.

My Wife Gloria

Gloria and her first husband, Caspar David Jorim, attended Bible school together in Port Moresby, Papua New Guinea (PNG), a close northern neighbour to Australia. They began their full time biblical studies in 1991. After three years their diligence in Christ was rewarded by the AOG church directorate. They served as senior pastors of the AOG churches in the region for the next ten years (1994–2004). Gloria remembers her husband as a black man with a 'white man's heart'. Women are second rate underdogs in some circles of PNG society and may get beaten into submission by some husbands, even if they are Christian or a pastor's wife. PNG males who paid a bride price treat their wives as articles of purchase, like a car they just acquired needing repair. Gloria says that its deep rooted in the culture of some of the islanders. Fortunately, Gloria's children did not insist on a bride price from me.

When Caspar died through severe liver failure, it was suspected by her family that a close relative had put a curse on him because of jealousy. This, unfortunately, is not uncommon practice by some PNG individuals even if they are Christians. Incredible that Christians would do that, isn't it? Papua New Guineans are a fearful people in general and suspect witchcraft at play whenever their health or physical welfare unexpectedly declines.

They are very careful who they shake hands with or invite into their house. A jealous 'friend' may even secretly stuff gravel down their toilet drain on a visit. In Thessalonica, Greece, 'Harry the man of God', has a powerful international prophetic, teaching and healing ministry. Scoan Thessalonica, is worth watching on YouTube. In one session he warned his followers not to accept a bottle of water from just anybody. It may have prayers and curses targeted against Christians attached; related testimonies were convincing. He explained that physical items can become spiritual vehicles carrying a blessing or a curse. When handkerchiefs or aprons, the apostle Paul's skin had touched, were passed around people got healed (Acts 19:11-12). We don't think about that in the developed nations, do we?

We shake hands freely, accept gifts of food, and display items on our walls and shelves at home such as memorabilia from our travels to exotic countries. Gruesome masks from Asia and the Pacific islands are copies of demons that satanic devotees have seen in trances. Paul commanded all such things to be burned, not to be passed on as we tend to do in our donations to charity stores today,

"Many of them also which used curious arts brought their books together and burned them before all men: and they counted the price of them, and found it fifty thousand pieces of silver" (Acts 19:19, KJV).

Gloria gave me examples of the power of witchcraft among Christians in PNG, which at first, I was reluctant to believe. It is difficult for the PNG Christian to believe that they are the temple of the Holy Spirit, God Himself, and that curses of any kind are therefore ineffective (Luke 10:19). This is the environment in which most of them have grown up in. Christian women remain fearful all their lives of jealous PNG Christian rivals, even if they live overseas. Strange but true!

Complacent western Christians have much to learn according to Gloria. We can unwittingly become victims of demons if we don't take such things more seriously. Satan has been celebrating his influence over Australia far too long which make Australians unusually resistant to the gospel. There are satanists praying every day for the breakdown of Christian marriages with apparent success according to statistics. Friends of mine came across a Sydney woman lost in prayer on a Hyde Park bench. Thinking they found a soul mate they shrunk back when she said that she was praying for Christian marriages to fail!

When Gloria's husband died, the callous male board of their AOG church directed her to leave the manse the very next day. *"But where will I go with my two children? I have no income or funds to support ourselves"* she said. Nevertheless, the board and pastors insisted that she must leave to one of their residences where she would have to pay rent. She could have had support from some, but she decided to keep it a private matter in case it started inter-tribal conflicts. Gloria fought tenaciously for her right as the ex-Senior Pastor to remain in the manse until she could provide an income for herself and her children. Australian pastors have retirement benefits but there is no such equivalent in PNG.

One day a police unit with guns raised surrounded their house. A group of three pastors acted like a pack of dogs on a leash repeatedly shouting, *"Get out - You*

MERGING JEW AND GENTILE FOR PERFECTION

have no right to be here". Gloria's young daughter hid under the bed afraid of being shot. Emmanuel, Gloria's teenage son, confronted the armed men and said, "*I am not a tenant. My father was the senior pastor here. My mother has a theological diploma from the AOG church and is a pastor here. We are not tenants to be thrown out. I belong here.*" The armed men were astounded and withdrew.

Soon after, two of the pastors returned, this time with a dog squad. She later found out that the third pastor did not come because he was ashamed that he had taken part, saying "*I would not want my wife to be treated that way if I died.*" The two pastors howled threats as before. Fearing for her children Gloria stepped outside. Some members of the dog squad were of the same tribe and recognized their former pastor. They laid down their weapons. Gloria explained what it was all about. The commander handed over to Gloria a fistful of eviction papers the church had given them and left the premises. Gloria explained that not all AOG churches are like that, but that often the wrong men get voted in because of tribal rivalry. PNG has 800 separate language groups. Some of the tribes have very different facial characteristics according to their ancient origins so there is little desire for national peace and unity by some.

The board continued to hassle Gloria through the law courts, but the civil court ruled against the church every time. The church Superintendent even forbid her to use the water on the premises and made life difficult for her. They had no source of income excepts for some money a family gave to support Ruth's education at university. Emmanuel sacrificed his own studies and lived on Gloria's home-baked rolls for breakfast, lunch, and dinner. Occasionally, another poor widow would join them bringing some rice and a can of fish which they would all share. Subsequently many of her belongings were stolen. The church Superintendent held the keys. According to police investigations, it was an inside job. Amazingly, Gloria keeps on forgiving them.

The family underwent five years of severe hardship. Not surprisingly, Gloria became angry with God. One day at a church service, a woman filled with the Holy Spirit came over to Gloria and laughed in her face saying, "*The Lord knows that you are fit enough to face your problems.*" She was offended but then realized it was from God. A word came to Gloria afterwards,

"In the things that you have suffered the most, you shall shine the brightest."

It is then that Gloria realized that God had allowed this suffering to prepare her for whatever the future held. At a meeting in 2011, she heard a sermon on Genesis 1:26 which proclaims that God had given dominion over all the animals to Adam and Eve. Secondly, that God had given man dominion over the Earth including all raw materials brought into existence by a creative word from God. Hearing other sermons on Jesus stilling the sea and a fig tree to wither and die, she began to literally believe in the declarations of Genesis 1:26–28 and Psalm 8:4–8. Her prayers changed in tone. She took onboard every promise discussed at conferences in PNG and during her brief ministry visits to Australia. Gloria says, *"I would get up early to speak to the creation about my position on the Earth as a ruler having dominion over the creation."* God granted her desire.

Her prayers initially focused on her hard times especially on the lack of finance. She spoke directly to God expecting Him to answer, *"Since you took my husband from me, it's up to you to provide for us"* and left the whole matter in the hands of God.

One day, after having heard more sermons based on Genesis 1:26, she took command of the situation believing that as a child of God she had authority to rule over the earth. She looked at the two *Kinas* in her purse and spoke gently to the money. Gloria commanded the notes to bring their fellow notes to her. Soon after, a lady was about to put her tithes into the offering box when God put it in her mind to give the money to Gloria instead. Gloria thanked God, and the two *Kinas*, and inserted the notes alongside the two *Kinas* in her purse.

She prayed similarly for a top job with the government. She had much teaching experience but now asked, or rather commanded, the system to provide her with a job. A high-paying job was offered as a trainer with Urban Youth Unemployment funded by the World Bank through a German Bank paying 300 *Kinas*, the equivalent of AUD$150 per day. With the proceeds, she eventually travelled for two weeks with her two teenage children to Jerusalem where they planted three olive trees. Gloria kept much of her success a secret in case jealousy, even among her closest friends, would give rise to harm. She only shares God's blessings with her children's families.

Gloria did not keep the income for herself but set up her son in business which also became very successful, to such a degree that in a fit of envy, one of Gloria's brothers put a curse on Gloria's son Emmanuel to die. One day while Emmanuel was driving his car, he saw a pair of hands grab him and set him on the ground outside. Within seconds, his car rolled over into a mass of torn metal. Such is the power of witchcraft whenever Christians mix Christianity with local beliefs. Charles believes that they become prisoners of their own fears. Scripture warns that whatever one sows (or believes), he/she will also reap (Galatians 6:7). I have no hesitation to believe my stepson's testimony because I once felt the five-fingered hand of an invisible angel save me from certain electrocution as I explained on my website (www.creation6000.com).

Together with her son, Gloria set up '*Voice of Hope Mission*' through which they were able to help some widows immigrate and obtain jobs in Australia (James 2:14-20). Her son gave her a special thank-you gift for her fiftieth birthday in 2014—an expensive brand-new car which she had to leave behind in PNG when she came over to join me ten years later. Gloria left all her worldly goods in PNG and came empty handed to

Australia to marry me. Her son is equally generous and gave many of his assets, including cash, to the needy.

Gloria loves to recount another astounding miracle of her many interactions with nature. They lived on a property with a large tree near the house that daily shed an enormous number of leaves. Sweeping up the leaves became a tedious task. A frustrated Gloria commanded the tree to stop shedding its leaves. Her children, Ruth and Emmanuel, ran to her excitedly the next day with the news that there wasn't a single leaf lying on the ground. This continued for three months until Gloria decided that it was time for the obedient tree to return to its normal cycles. She prayed for the tree to resume its normal growth cycle. After two days, Gloria noticed yellowing of leaves on the tree and leaves dropping once again.

This reminded me of the remarkable encounter Jesus had with a fig tree that bore no fruit and the seemingly impossible promise that his disciples would one day be able to fulfil similar miracles (Mark 11:13–14, 20–23). The reader will recall that the fig tree thereupon withered and died surprising his disciples. Jesus explained that this was a prophetic outcome because Israel was as the fig tree, unable to bear fruit in its time, and would spiritually die to make room for the *Times of the Gentiles* or *The Overspreading of Abominations* (Daniel Chapter 9, KJV); a 2000-year period during which the gospel would come to the Gentiles instead, and that they would bear godly fruit. This period is about to come to an end as God is turning his attention to Israel once again as prophesied in Daniel Chapter 9 (The 70-week Prophecy).

Having experienced so much success because of intense prayer, Gloria began to accept the prophecies over her that one day, because of all the sufferings she had endured, she would marry a man who would elevate her to new heights.

Gloria and I believe that the Earth will bring catastrophes upon unbelievers as detailed in the book of Revelation (the 7 vials) because they had mistreated the environment and mocked the gospel for so long. Historical records demonstrate that whenever God punished Israel for its rebellion, the land and its animals suffered likewise. This principle is firmly established in the Word of God and will surely come to pass upon a rebellious world according to the will of God. God warned Israel to be careful because, if they became disobedient, the Promised Land would spit them out. Hear the various translations all of which make the land the active object,

"Lest the land vomit you out when you make it unclean, as it vomited out the nation that was before you" and *"So do not defile the land and <u>give it a reason</u> to vomit you out, as it will vomit out the people who live there now"* (Leviticus 18:28). Interesting wording that I never thought about before, isn't it? The CEV puts it this way, *"Then the land won't become sick of you and vomit you up, just as it did them"*. **God obviously created nature with an ability to respond to the spiritual status of its inhabitants.**

Gloria occasionally conducts spiritual warfare with intense prayers. She has experienced dark figures leaning over her bed, making it difficult for her to breathe. The figures flee upon her pleading the blood of Jesus. Gloria believes the apostolic word that the weapons of our warfare are not carnal, but spiritual. Gloria verbalizes the word of God, gives praise to God in worship and has used covenant salt as did Elisha in 2 Kings 2:20-21. Gloria used to blow her shofar in PNG as a sign of victory and delivery (Luke 4:18). Prophecies concerning her came to pass even as they have come to pass for me!

Gloria's Children Confirm
Gloria's Prayer Outcomes

Ruth was a university student while Emmanuel was a year-12 student when they witnessed the outcome of Gloria's two outstanding prayers. Ruth writes, "Trusting the Lord with our life's journey was significant having been raised in a Christian home. It was astounding watching my mother pray daily and declaring the Word of God over our lives, in and around the surroundings of our house.

I can vividly remember in early 2007, that mum declared this Bible scripture in our home. Genesis 1: 26 *"And God said, let us make man in our image, after our likeness: and let them have dominion over the fish of the sea, and over the fowl of the air, and over the cattle, and over all the earth, and over every creeping thing that creeps on the earth"* (MKJV).

Both my younger brother and I were living at home and would observe our mum with some amazement. She would wake up in the early mornings and pray around our home. Then she would rake the leaves from the trees in front our house. There was a particular tree right in front of our door that dropped many leaves every day. Mum swept the path daily to ensure that the entrance to our home would always be welcoming.

One morning after clearing the steps and path she addressed the tree and told it to stop dropping its leaves causing her to do a lot of work daily. I stood in amazement before leaving to go to the university. She spoke to the tree as though it could hear! I did not understand what my mum was doing however I watched with curiosity to see what the outcome would be.

The next morning before I left the house, I circled the tree to check if it had obeyed my mum's instruction. I saw no leaves on the ground, but I was not sure if it had listened to my mum. For the next three months, however, I checked the tree daily before leaving for university. The tree never had a single yellow leaf on it. The tree's leaves were always green, and I could see the power of the spoken Word of God based on Genesis 1:26. There is power in the Word of God when you trust and believe it with faith; the spoken Word of God will come alive.

Three months later mum walked out one morning and called my younger brother and I to witness her command the tree to return to its normal seasonal cycle. The very next day the tree dropped its first yellow leaves. It had returned to its normal cycle.

Around the same time, we had vehicles entering our premises to visit a pastor's family who lived downstairs in the mission house we were in. We had incidents of these visitors disrespecting and trying to instil fear in us because they knew our dad was no longer there to defend us after God had called him home. We would find out that they would gossip bad things against my mum to the pastor who didn't like us anyway. [PNG males disrespect women in general comments Charles. The word got around that Gloria was the worst case of a female confronting male pastors. She had stood up against the church for 5 years refusing to be evicted].

Mum, after seeing the power of Genesis 1:26 earlier, decided to speak to the ground commanding the dirt road to obey her. She told the earth within the premises to give ear to her wishes and commanded the grounds that any person driving into our premises with bad intentions would immediately have car problems. It was a while before we had a visitor into the premises.

The vehicle entered the driveway in good running condition. However, when the visitor decided to leave, he was not able to start his car. The ignition of the car clicked but the power was not enough to start the engine. When the car was manually rolled out of the grounds it would start again. People were startled when this occurred repeatedly with other visitors. The word soon got around to avoid our place.

My younger brother, Emmanuel, witnessed all these events. He confirmed them to Charles over the phone by sending his photo to include in Ruth's letter. In one instance he ran downstairs to help them push their vehicle out the front gate. Once the car was outside it started easily and could be driven off. Visitors were frightened off from coming again". Praise the Lord.

CHAPTER 5

Gloria and Charles

Gloria's ancestors, including her grandparents, were demon worshippers. Along with many others she used to chew betel nuts that contain a mild stimulant, arouse awareness, and suppress hunger. Betel nuts turn the mouth a repulsive fleshy red, ugly to watch on Youtube. Her family was extremely poor until her husband encouraged her to convert to Christ. Gloria had a wonderful first marriage to Casper. God prospered Gloria and her family until her husband passed away.

When her daughter Ruth came down to Australia for Gloria's marriage to me, Ruth wrote a touching farewell to her mother following her brief stay in Cairns. She reminded her mother how they used to struggle financially for years before God prospered the family. Ruth recounted how her brother sacrificed himself to eat baked buns for breakfast, lunch, and dinner so that she could receive her university education. Gloria cried as she read the letter and remembered her difficult years.

Gloria never wanted to remarry once her husband and co-pastor passed into glory. He was an unusually loving and caring man, both in his marriage and in the church. Gloria and I sometimes laugh because there are so many PNG widows hoping to find white husbands in Australia. Their former husbands had treated them brutally in Papua New Guinea (PNG).

A very close friend of mine confirmed how men generally treat women in New Britain, PNG. David and his wife served as missionaries in northern PNG on a remote island where they built a Bible School. They loved PNG, and every time I make mention of tropical fruits David's wife yearns to be back in PNG. During their stay it was much more peaceful than it is now. Today there are occasional violent clashes often initiated by from those in the highlands who have spread into the cities seeking jobs. David recounted an incident during one of his sermons to his male Christian converts. The title of his sermon? *"Do not lift a hand against a woman"*. The audience murmured and became distressed as he preached. My friend stopped and asked, *"What have I said that's wrong?"* Some of the men called out respectfully, *"We all beat up our wives. How else will they submit to us?"* That sums up the PNG mindset of many.

Revenge killings and cursing each other by witchcraft, known as voodoo in the Caribbean, is a common feature of life which is ingrained in a sizeable fraction of the PNG Christian community. Gloria fears it and is wary who she speaks to. Her own sibling brother used curses attempting to kill Gloria's granddaughter and son out of jealousy. Her husband's brother did it too for the same reason. This is inconceivable to the average Australian. I initially couldn't come to terms with it. How could a Christian, or even a non-Christian sibling for that matter, send a curse upon their own biological brother or sister, I asked myself.

Then I remembered Balaam a prophet of God who was very intimate with the Lord. As Israel was wandering through the Promised Land Balaam was about to put a curse on Israel from the top of a hill on behalf of Balak, King of Moab. Balak had offered him gold and silver. Despite the Lord forbidding Balaam, Balaam repeatedly asked the Lord because he desired the reward money. When he set out once again to curse Israel with the intention of setting up altars for best outcomes, a donkey with a man's voice stopped him. Had the donkey not stopped, the angel the donkey saw would have killed Balaam.

This is serious stuff. God was displeased with Balaam because it seems to me that his curse, since he was an anointed prophet of God, would have harmed the progress of the Hebrews through Canaan by giving opportunities to the enemy (Numbers chapters 22-24). When the Lord spends four chapters on a matter it deserves attention. Numbers 22:6 is a critical verse, the King of Moab saying, "*So come right now and curse this people for me, because there are too many of them for me to handle. Perhaps I'll be able to strike them down and drive them out of the land, since I know that whomever you bless is blessed and whomever you curse is cursed*" (GNB). That verifies the belief of Christians in Papua New Guinea. I doubt whether Gentile Christians have given it much thought. I certainly never have until I met Gloria!

Gloria developed strong convictions of her own. Gloria is convinced that her husband died through witchcraft carried out by a member of his family which I am now prepared to believe. Having suffered herself she desires to minister to widows and orphans and has sacrificed her worldly goods to her children and the needy. I have been ministering to Gloria, for her to give priority to the power and glory of the Holy Spirit and not to be entangled with the spirit of fear. Jesus is our burden-bearer (Proverbs 3:5-6; 1 Peter 5:7). God does not expect us to carry another person's load; instead to pray for them and bring our own anxieties to the foot of the cross. *"For every man shall bear his own burden"* (Galatians 6:5).

Gloria's Contributions to My Faith

The apostle Paul commended corporate communion but was distressed how disorderly it had become in the Corinthian church where responsible oversight was obviously lacking. Gloria loves to take communion frequently and appreciates having communion whenever it is offered in church. She also likes to take communion at home. After Pentecost the New Testament church pattern was to break bread from house to house (Acts 2:46). This could indicate either having fellowship meals between households or perhaps the apostles or some heads of houses bringing communion to every house. We have assumed that the latter might have some truth in it. In either case, it doesn't really matter and can only be beneficial. I have therefore agreed for us to celebrate communion at home and at church.

When my own parents were sick and had not attended church for months I took communion to their home. My mother had been in a state of poor health for years suffering from anxiety attacks because the distended hernia of her stomach often interfered with her heartbeat. They appreciated the communion I brought. The next morning, I heard that she had passed away during the night from a heart attack. The Lord's timing was amazing because I hadn't seen them for a month but felt a sudden urge to visit them.

My mother had been continually fearful of dying. She regularly visited a hypnotherapist to ease her mind. I tried to discourage her attendance, but she refused to listen. The afternoon I visited she told me something when my father left the room. "*I must tell you something. The last time I visited the hypnotherapist I was sitting in the dim room with his gentle voice almost putting me to sleep. Suddenly his voice changed to a deep tone and growled at me: 'I am the devil talking to you.' I leapt out of the chair and fled from his office.*"

Gloria's main contribution to my faith has been to convince me that demonic spirits are very active responding to people harbouring jealousy. The devil is particularly delighted whenever he is empowered by embittered Christians. I once heard of the jealousy of a senior pastor towards a rapidly rising junior star which caused difficulties. The budding junior left the congregation. Who knows what the senior pastor or the junior prospect might next be tempted to do?

I met a Brazilian man at liberty to preach and minister healing but only at Brazilian branches of the AOG. After he prayed for my knee, I asked him why not? "*Jealousy*" was the curt reply. The Lord's shepherds are not always the Lord's shepherds. That was a hard lesson for me to learn over the first 30 years as a young Christian.

PNG Christians are plagued with violence and family reprisals for the same reason, sometimes even between the families of pastors, especially if they are from different tribes of which there are hundreds. Jealous family members do not hesitate to use curses and witchcraft to destroy their own flesh and blood. I would not have believed had I not heard it personally from Gloria who is an extremely devoted Christian. Her husband, a loving senior pastor, was the victim of curses from his own brother. Gloria has convinced me of that, something which I couldn't have ever believed before until I was beginning to experience spiritual attacks myself as I will shortly explain. I believe that the Lord has been wanting an opportunity to teach me for a long time.

Though Gloria has an intimate relationship with the Lord through much prayer she seals her lips about any good fortune coming her way out of fear that others, including Christians and Christian pastors, might be tempted to use witchcraft to spoil her blessings. Can you believe that? It's true unfortunately, as I am finding out daily! A West Indian Christian wife of a good friend of mine in Melbourne confirmed that this is also the case amongst her people in the Caribbean islands south of Mexico. That's why she avoids being friends with people of her own nation.

Satan has bound the entire PNG nation with a spirit of fear. When I got to know Gloria, I confronted her with typical western superiority about superstitious nonsense which she should just ignore — no curse could influence anyone filled with the Holy Spirit, or so I thought.

I Learned About Spiritual Warfare from Gloria

I was born-again when I awoke in bed on Easter Monday morning in 1976 with a wonderful experience that resembled what happened to the 120 disciples on the Jewish day of Pentecost (Acts Chapter 2 and my website www.creation6000.com). I was blessed with a love for the Word of God. A few weeks later I was water baptised by full immersion in a church. The Lord allowed me to witness a couple of stunning miraculous healings there including healing of dental cavities through prayer. As a scientist my jaw dropped with awe. The Lord next gave me numerous promises and warnings about my future through visions and dreams, especially during the first few years of my Christian walk (*Immortal to the End: A Challenging True Story of the Supernatural*, Bookside Press, 2024). I was fortunate that the Lord gave me a precious life-long mentor, Gordon together with his wife Dorothy, who secured me in my early years which were scary because my wife didn't take kindly to my constant attendance at Bible studies.

Despite having the experience of being filled with the Spirit, I never dared to talk to nature as though it should obey me. Gloria does! Not only that, but PNG Christian culture allows them to believe that anyone who sets a curse on someone else invites a demonic spirit to work on its victim, usually in the form of an animal should the spirit reveal itself. This is not anti-scriptural because the dragon, the beast and his false prophet manifest unclean spirits in the shape of frogs (Revelation 16:13-14).

One day after I married Gloria, she told me in the morning of a dark demonic figure that approached her bed trying to smother her while I was sleeping in an adjoining room. She rebuked it sternly by claiming the blood of Jesus multiple times. I still found it difficult to believe that anything like that could happen to a devoted Christian like her, so I reminded her that the Holy Spirit dwells in us and that she had nothing to fear, thinking at the same time how dreadfully superstitious PNG Christians are.

A few days later, the Lord taught me a lesson and allowed me to experience two demonic attacks which woke me up sweating with fear. He was teaching me that demons especially target Christians who mean business with God. Satan doesn't bother pew-warming complacent Christians. Naming the blood of Jesus and our obedience to the Word is Satan's greatest fear and weapon against him. As the apostle Paul said, we do not wrestle against flesh and blood but against powerful unseen supernatural beings in high places and that our weapons must not be carnal responses for the devil laughs at them (2 Corinthians 10:2-7).

Satan tempted Jesus three times when Jesus was at his weakest point having already fasted without quenching his thirst for many days in the wilderness. Satan knows the scriptures better than most of us and tries to thwart the prophecies in Chapter 12 and onwards in the book of Revelation. Not only will he lose access to the second heaven then and be cast to the earth, but 3½ years later he will be chained for 1000 years during the Millennium and then be cast into the eternal Lake of Fire. The rich man who never helped Lazarus, who was daily begging at his gate, experienced only a foretaste of hell in Sheol (Luke 16:19-31, Gehenna in Greek). Gehenna was Israel's best example to imagine what hell is like. It was the Valley of Hinnom outside the walls of Jerusalem where Israel burned children to the Ammonite god Moloch.

How did the Lord convince me that I had to take spiritual warfare seriously? One evening during our month-long honeymoon in Victoria we were driving home on a dark moonlit night to our timeshare unit in the countryside. Coming into the gravel lane about 100 metres from our parking spot I nearly ran over an owl squatting in the middle of the road starring straight at me. I braked to a halt not wanting to kill it. It twisted its head now and then as though it was mounted on ball bearings. I was speechless! Gloria said it's an owl. I know it's an owl, I thought, but having never seen one in the wild in all my 84 years fascinated me. It just looked straight at me. It's an owl, she exclaimed again. Yes, an owl. How unusual, I thought.

I was about to run the engine louder to scare it out of the way when it suddenly took off silently into the night to my right. As it took off there was a very loud bang on my side of the car. I saw nothing, not a bird nor a kangaroo. The owl hadn't touched it. I couldn't work out what was happening. I just sat in the car speechless. Gloria exclaimed a third time, "*It's an owl, a bird of the night!*" Yes, I thought, it's an owl. So what? Except that I had never come across one before. I couldn't understand why Gloria kept repeating herself.

I went peacefully to sleep that night but then had a nightmare. I dreamt that I was in an old log cabin, a ranch like one sees in western movies. Someone was trying to come into the cabin during the middle of the night. I feared for my family. I frantically rushed around looking for boards to barricade the doors and windows; I must protect them. I woke up with my heart pounding with fear but couldn't lose the thought that I must protect my family. The thought kept me awake for some time. A warning from God that something was about to happen, I wondered. Then another anxiety attack came upon me. I should stop writing this book and go to the university library instead, to catch up on the last 20 years of scientific publications. There was an important scientific paper I could still write. It dawned on me that demons were trying to distract and delay me. I rebuked the spirit of distraction. Eventually, I went to sleep again. The next morning, I told Gloria and that we needed to pray.

"I wasn't surprised" she calmly said. *"You saw an owl. I immediately realized last night that you were going to face a spiritual attack, and you did! I didn't tell you because you would not have believed me."*

But why was there a loud bang on the car door? The owl hadn't even touched it, I told Gloria. She then said, *"That wasn't an animal we saw. It was a monitoring spirit. It's telling you that you are being watched for a potential break-through attack. Had you run over the owl the person who inspired the demonic attack would have been killed"*. I couldn't believe what she was saying, but I knew I had experienced something very real. Who or what sharply banged my side of the car so loudly when the owl took off? It wasn't a kangaroo or bird.

The following day when I woke up, I saw in my mind the owl's face in detail. I couldn't shake free from it. As I was watching it morphed into the face of a woman who had made subtle advances to me only months ago. I called out her name. I had been ignoring her obvious signals for months. I then remembered Joseph's experience in Egypt when Potiphar's wife tried to seduce him, but he fled from the scene. Her intense lust for Joseph turned to hate. She lied to her husband and Joseph ended up in prison.

Through Gloria's experiences in PNG and believable explanations I finally had to concede that spiritual warfare and demonic attacks are real (2 Corinthians 10:3-4). Gloria explained to me that when her husband's brother cursed him, owls surrounded their house the night he passed away.

"But, but" I said, *"the woman's face I saw was an Australian pastor"*. That's not uncommon in PNG she retorted. *"But how could a Christian put a curse on me?"*. I knew the answer before I even opened my mouth.

It made me think of Balaam God's false prophet who was willing to betray Israel for reward.

I thank the Lord that he had been waiting for the right time to convince me of that; no matter how weird it may seem to ordinary Christians. I had been praying for years to receive the gift of discerning spirits and authority to deal with demons influencing the church.

Some weeks later we were in a shopping centre. We walked out of Kmart and there right in front of me was a shirt with an imprint of a large owl looking at me. Gloria said, "*It's an owl!*" Oh no, I thought. This time she really is being superstitious. But guess what? When we got to our SUV the window on the top of the car was fully open and the window on the driver's side was fully down. The car was getting drenched. I couldn't believe it. I hadn't done that. It's never happened to me before. Gloria reminded me, "*You saw the owl, didn't you?*" I got the message. We prayed before we drove off.

As Joseph Prince says on TV, the devil will deceive and attack even Holy Spirit-filled people.

People Can be Endowed with Demonic Power

Christians need to become more aware of the reality of powerful spiritual forces especially in lackadaisical, unconcerned Australia. I remember being allocated the 1952 book "*Seven Years in Tibet*" by the German Heinrich Harrer for essential reading in year-12 way back in 1956. The book influenced many of us to practice some form of spiritualism such as participating in seances. I did. Heinrich escaped British arrest in India during WWII by crossing into Tibet where he became the personal friend of the Dalai Lama for a number of years. According to Heinrich some devout Tibetan priests could, amongst other things, levitate impressing all of us to try and do likewise but without success. However, the deed was done. We had opened ourselves not only to the spirit-world, but we devoured books on the dark side. Two of us attempted suicide a year or two later.

Like myself, Australian churches have long been partially blind to the reality of fallen angels wanting to destroy Christians. Moses and Aaron had to battle against real wizards in Pharaoh's court. The wizards were able to spiritually transform their rods into real snakes. Books like the *Harry Potter* series glorify their power immunizing fans from the evil intent of demonic activity. It has reached the stage whether what we do or believe will mean either hell or heaven.

Devilish activity is not harmless. In the book of Job, Satan killed not only Job's 10 children through natural disasters but also many of Job's servants in the field by inciting roving bandits to plunder their herds. The Lord did not intervene. He allowed the trial to eventually increase Job's trust in the Lord. The number 10 happens to be Bible code for a trial. The Lord had been in control all the time. He told Satan that he could do anything to Job except to take his life. You may remember that in return he rewarded Job with a double portion and wonderful children. But for him to have lost his first children bothers Charles to this day. Abraham was tested too, but in his case, he received Isaac back alive. As the old adage goes, 'God works in strange ways.'

As described previously in this book, when persons yield themselves to the devil astonishing things can happen. In voodoo practices in the Carribean people acquire some item belonging to the person they wish harm and create a doll that wears that item, it being a sample of hair or a shred of clothing. They next pray and go into a trance pushing needles into the doll where they want the person harmed. The victim actually suffers. PNG citizens can do the same by placing a curse on others.

Australian indigenous aborigines 'point a bone' to an adversary or relative they want to kill. The victim becomes weak and wants to die. They lie down in a secluded place and actually die. It is very real. The Australian native practices spiritual witchcraft when they perform night corrobborees hidden from outside eyes. They dance around a fire stamping their feet and chant to the sound of drumsticks and digeridoos. At the centre is a powerful member of the community dancing around with a stick. As the corrobboree intensifies, they watch on with great interest. When the stick begins to dance on its own without it being held, they know that they made contact. Examine whether you have any such items in your home as novelties. It is possible that they exert some form of control over your household.

We both heard this testimony recently. A PNG pastor had been trying to break up a couple's mixed marriage. One day the husband called home that he seriously injured the side of his head. The next day the pastor called while she was alone and asked her, "*How are you?*". "*Not very good. My husband hurt the side of his head filling his mouth with blood*". Hearing that the visitor said, "*That's what I wanted to hear*" and turned around without any words of comfort or consolation. He drove off without even saying goodbye. "*Did not even Satan marvellously transform himself into an angel of light? Therefore, it is no great thing if his ministers also transform themselves as ministers of righteousness, whose end shall be according to their works.*" (2 Corinthians 11:14-15).

It's important for the Word to take precedence in our lives rather than personal experiences. There is no doubt that demons target people that endanger his desire to eventually rule over the Earth. We are to clothe ourselves with the whole armour of God (Ephesians 6:10-18). We would not have been given those exhortations if spiritual attacks were only a figment of our imagination. An article on www. crosswalk.com makes the additional important point that "*the Bible makes a distinction between trials, tribulations, and temptations. The first is when God allows difficulties so we can draw closer to Him; the second is when hardships come by way of the world being fallen* [by chance events]. *Temptation is when the Devil and evil, or the power of the flesh, try to lead people away from God. Some people make the mistake of assuming that any difficulty they face is an attack, and that it needs to be dealt with as spiritual warfare. Understanding the difference between the three is important, and it is crucial to use prayer and the Bible to discern what is happening when there is hardship*". The desire for reality and balance is the message of our book.

Nothing Can Withstand the Will of God

"*My times are in Your hand; Deliver me from the hand of my enemies, And from those who persecute me*" (Psalm 31:15, NKJV).

Having acknowledged that we are fighting spiritual powers in high places, and that the devil can create havoc in people's lives, our eyes remain fastened upon Jesus. Worthy is the Lamb that has overcome the world (John 16:33) and "*They overcame him by the blood of the Lamb, and by the word of their testimony; and they loved not their lives unto the death*", (Revelation 12:11, ERV).

Nothing on earth or in heaven can shorten our lives if we are truly in Him. Whatever powers, hateful crowds or supernatural forces were against him, nothing could extinguish the life of Jesus on earth until the set time appointed by the Father. Time and time again Jesus vanished from vile crowds because *"His time was not yet"* (John 2:4; 7:6-8, 30; 8;20).

"If God is for us, no one can stand against us. And God is with us", (Romans 8:31, ERV).

Moses and Aaron walked undaunted past the evil wizards of Pharaoh. Elisha's dry bones in an open sepulchre brought life to a body hastily discarded upon his bones (2 Kings 13:20-21). Jeremiah remained faithful to the Lord though everyone of influence around him was killed during the Babylonian captivity. Jesus remained faithful and surrendered his life to the Father whereupon he rose again. None of these men died natural deaths because they were on missions from the Father. Nothing can defy the power of the Holy Spirit!

Charles keeps on walking undaunted through the many trials he faces because the Lord promised him long life to the very end, by a small voice of the Lord and in visions. Charles belittles demonic forces, though they be painful, uncomfortable, and inconvenient, considering them as distractions. He believes that he is one of many walking temples of the Holy Spirit (1 Corinthians 6:19) and that nothing can touch him fatally, neither witchcraft nor anything, because he is a purchased possession of Christ. Nevertheless, Charles will always appreciate the prayers of Gloria and others. Remembering that all prophecies are filled with symbolisms, we finish this section with a promise and blessing upon faithful 'Spiritual Israel' from Isaiah, Chapter 60 (BBE),

"Up! let your face be bright, for your light has come, and the glory of the Lord is shining on you. For truly, the earth will be dark, and the peoples veiled in blackest night; but the Lord will be shining on you, and his glory will be seen among you. And nations will come to your light, and kings to your bright dawn. Let your eyes be lifted up and see: they are all coming together to you: your sons will come from far, and your daughters taken with loving care. Then you will see, and be bright with joy, and your heart will be shaking with increase of delight: for the produce of the sea will be turned to you, the wealth of the nations will come to you. You will be full of camel-trains, even the young camels of Midian and Ephah; all from Sheba will come, with gold and spices, giving word of the great acts of the Lord. All the flocks of Kedar will come together

to you, the sheep of Nebaioth will be ready for your need; they will be pleasing offerings on my altar, and my house of prayer will be beautiful.

Who are these coming like a cloud, like a flight of doves to their windows? Vessels of the sea-lands are waiting for me, and the ships of Tarshish first, so that your sons may come from far, and their silver and gold with them, to the place of the name of the Lord your God, and to the Holy One of Israel, because he has made you beautiful.

Men from strange countries will be building up your walls, and their kings will be your servants: for in my wrath I sent punishment on you, but in my grace I have had mercy on you. Your doors will be open at all times; they will not be shut day or night; so that men may come into you with the wealth of the nations, with their kings at their head. For the nation or kingdom which will not be your servant will come to destruction; such nations will be completely waste.

The glory of Lebanon will come to you, the cypress, the plane, and the sherbin-tree together, to make my holy place beautiful; and the resting-place of my feet will be full of glory. And the sons of those who were cruel to you will come before you with bent heads; and those who made sport of you will go down on their faces at your feet; and you will be named, The Town [City] of the Lord, The Zion of the Holy One of Israel. Though you were turned away from, and hated, and had no helper, I will make you a pride for ever, a joy from generation to generation. You will take the milk of the nations, flowing from the breast of kings; and you will see that I, the Lord, am your saviour, and he who takes up your cause, the Strong One of Jacob.

In place of brass, I will give gold, and for iron silver, and for wood brass, and for stones iron: and I will make Peace your judge, and Righteousness your overseer. Violent acts will no longer be seen in your land, wasting or destruction in your limits; but your walls will be named, Salvation, and your doors Praise. The sun will not be your light by day, and the moon will no longer be bright for you by night: but the Lord will be to you an eternal light, and your God your glory. Your sun will never again go down, or your moon keep back her light: for the Lord will be your eternal light, and the days of your sorrow will be ended.

Your people will all be upright, the land will be their heritage forever; the branch of my planting, the work of my hands, to be for my glory. The smallest of their families will become a thousand, and a small one a strong nation: I, the Lord, will make it come quickly in its time."

Body Ministry: The Key of David

Gloria and her husband were the Senior Pastors of the AOG church in the district of Port Moresby. In contrast to her praising the AOG church she and her husband oversaw, body ministry was never employed at church. It is foreign to her and to pastors who sit at the helm.

Charles, however, believes in body ministry which became somewhat acceptable and was successful in the church he attended in Melbourne, Australia. Body ministry is where the congregation ministers one to another either during the main service or when people have been dismissed and they mingle with each other. Charles recounts how one day he noted a middle-aged couple come to the service. What Charles had never observed on previous occasions was her heavily arthritic hands. They sat behind Charles. Early in the service Charles turned around and said, "*Stay on after the service. We want to pray for your hands*".

When the service ended Charles called over a former elder and missionary, so the two of them prayed for her. As soon as they laid hands on her Charles' friend burst out with a word of knowledge, "*You have much anger in your heart*". The woman shrank back, "*Yes, I hate my mother and father*". David and Charles ended up praying for her anger to cease and her heart to be cleansed but they did not pray for her hands. The husband was glad and said that it's been unliveable at home because of her constant anger. The next Sunday Charles thought that she may not turn up out of embarrassment, but she did. She and her husband had smiles on their faces which became broader over the weeks.

We are slowly but surely learning from each other to bring balance and more godliness into our lives. We have earthly responsibilities, and we have heavenly responsibilities. Jesus said to pay our dues to Caesar what is Caesar's and to God what is God's. There must be a balance between the natural and the spiritual as well. In church we honour pastors, their dedication to serve and we appreciate their sermons, but the body must play its part (Colossians 3:16). We must also heed the laws of the land when they don't conflict with the Word.

> *"Then how is it, brothers? When you come together, each one of you has a psalm, has a teaching, has a tongue, has a revelation, has an interpretation. Let all things be for building up"*, (1 Corinthians 14:26).

Charles' definition of body ministry is to get close to people, chat with them, pray for them after a service or in the home. Even a providentially inspired phone call has been known to prevent someone from committing suicide. Home cell groups are a great place to start body ministry. Do you belong to one?

Too many leave it to the pastors or elders to do everything. Home visitations are left to pastors because they are the ones on salary. Pastors will burn out as many already have, especially once the great harvest of the Lord will come like a tsunami and overwhelm the few able to minister to them. Every member of the body of Christ urgently needs to be trained and equipped to meet current and future needs (Ephesians 4:12-16). Moses was virtually a *one-man band* trying to solve everyone's complaint. He grew weary until God told him to delegate complaints of lesser importance to 70 appointed heads (Numbers 11:23-24). What a relief that would be to our pastors if they did the same!

Being passive pew-warmers was not the pattern of the New Testament church. Most congregations today are timid, no, much stronger than that Charles says, they are paralysed. Unfortunately, some gifted pastors drift away from God's will by doing everything from the stage robbing the body of its ministry.

The 'Key of David' was for David to involve all the Levites in ministry and worship:

"*And the key of the house of David will I lay upon his shoulder; so he shall open, and none shall shut; and he shall shut, and none shall open*", (Isaiah 22:22). In ancient days a key meant the authority of government. The southern kingdom became the House of David after the other ten tribes split from them forming the northern kingdom under Jereboam. The verse below clearly demonstrates the Key the Lord gave to David.

"*Then Solomon offered burnt offerings unto the LORD on the altar of the LORD, which he had built before the porch, even after a certain rate every day, offering according to the commandment of Moses, on the sabbaths, and on the new moons, and on the solemn feasts, three times in the year, even in the feast of unleavened bread, and in the feast of weeks, and in the feast of tabernacles.*

And he appointed, according to the order of David his father, the courses of the priests to their service, and the Levites to their charges, to praise and minister before the priests, as the duty of every day required: the porters also by their courses at every gate: for so had David the man of God commanded. And they departed not from the commandment of the king unto the priests and Levites concerning any matter or concerning the treasures. Now all the work of Solomon was prepared unto the day of the foundation of the house of the LORD, and until it was finished. So, the house of the LORD was perfected", (2 Chronicles 8:12-16).

> *"It's judgment time for Christians. We're the first in line. If it starts with us, think what it's going to be like for those who refuse God's message?"* (1 Peter 4:17, MSG)

Many congregations refrain from ministering one to one another even at church. Yet we are supposed to be a priesthood of believers foreshadowed by the priestly Levites who served in the temples (1 Peter 2:5-9). We are to minister to one another with our worldly goods and with any spiritual gifts we may possess (Acts 2:42-47). As members of the body of Christ we have received diverse spiritual gifts from the Lord and are expected to exercise them for the benefit of the community (1 Corinthians Chapter 12).

What prevents us from unpacking what he has already given us? It's like a father giving his son the keys to a new car for his birthday. Disappointed, the father asks the next morning, "*What's wrong son? I'm surprised that you haven't told me and mum what you think about your present?*" "*I just can't believe that you would have given me such an expensive car, so I didn't have a look, but I loved your great card. Thanks Dad.*"

God calls servants of the Lord in every nation to repent from their timidity (being a 'chicken') or on the other extreme, their self-importance. Even the apostles had to confront each other at times. When the 120 received the gift of the Holy Spirit in the upper room on the Day of Pentecost they were anything but timid from then on and boldly confronted the highest authorities. Formal old-fashioned church models must go. European missionaries brought a demonic doctrine, especially to PNG, that cemented people into a two-class system; a rut of clergy versus laymen.

In Australia some churches make room for body ministry, but most do not which must surely grieve the Holy Spirit! Direction in the Word, order and some form of structure must, of course, be maintained — that's the job of leaderships.

Attitudes must change before the imminent coming of the Lord. Too many grieve at home about the way meetings are held. We must learn to bring a word of truth in love to draw our meetings closer to God. All of us are called to be kings and priests not just a select few (Ephesians 4:13, Revelation 1:6; 5:10; 20:6). The pyramid system of the church must go, whether it be a one-man band or a multiple eldership! Charles is fired up about this issue and can be blunt, while Gloria holds back and considers it improper to speak out. This surprises Charles because Gloria bravely fought the PNG male clergy tooth and nail during the years when they attempted to evict her from the manse.

CHAPTER 6

Merging Gentile and Jewish Christians: Perfection

CHARLES & GLORIA JORIM PALLAGHY

First Fruits: Link to Passover and Consecration of the First-born

It is crucial to our consideration of perfection presented in this book that we read the following passages in the Bible because the Lord shall never deviate from his shadow of heavenly things as presented to us in the Old Testament. It is crucial that we understand the principle of first fruits. After the last plague in the land of Egypt when the Lord killed the first born of man and beast, the Lord commanded Moses to keep the Feast of First Fruits, in Exodus Chapter 12, and said,

"Sanctify unto me all the firstborn, whatsoever opens the womb among the children of Israel, both of man and of beast: it is mine" (Exodus 13:2, MKJV)

"Therefore, know that Jehovah your God, He is God, the faithful God who keeps covenant and mercy with them that love Him and keep His commandments, to a thousand generations. He repays those who hate Him to their face, to destroy them. He will not be slow to repay him who hates Him. He will repay him to his face. You shall keep the commandments and the statutes and the judgments which I command you today, to do them. It shall be, because you listen to these judgments and keep and do

them, Jehovah your God shall keep to you the covenant and the mercy which He swore to your fathers. He will love you and bless you and multiply you. He will also bless the fruit of your womb, and the fruit of your land, your grain, and your wine, and your oil, the increase of your cattle, and the flocks of your sheep, in the land which He swore to your fathers to give you. You shall be blessed above all people. There shall not be male or female barren among you or among your cattle. Jehovah will take away from you all sickness and will put none of the evil diseases of Egypt which you know upon you. But He will lay them upon all who hate you", (Deuteronomy 7:9-1, MKJV).

"You shall bring the Levites before the tabernacle of the congregation. And you shall gather the whole assembly of the sons of Israel together. And you shall bring the Levites before Jehovah. And the sons of Israel shall put their hands upon the Levites. And Aaron shall offer the Levites before Jehovah for an offering of the sons of Israel, so that they may do the service of Jehovah. The Levites shall lay their hands upon the heads of the bulls. And you shall offer the one for a sin offering, and the other for a burnt offering, to Jehovah, to make an atonement for the Levites. You shall set the Levites before Aaron, and before his sons, and offer them for an offering to Jehovah. So you shall separate the Levites from among the sons of Israel. And the Levites

shall be Mine. After that the Levites shall go in to do the service of the tabernacle of the congregation. And you shall purify them and offer them for a wave offering. For they are wholly given to Me from among the sons of Israel, instead of those that open every womb. The first-born of all the sons of Israel, I have taken them to Me. For all the first-born of the sons of Israel are Mine, both man and animal. On the day that I struck every first-born in the land of Egypt I set them apart for Myself. I have taken the Levites for all the first-born of the sons of Israel. I have given the Levites as a gift to Aaron and to his sons from among the sons of Israel, to do the service of the sons of Israel in the tabernacle of the congregation, and to make an atonement for the sons of Israel, so that there may be no plague among the sons of Israel when the sons of Israel come near the sanctuary", (Numbers 8:9-19).

Hannah, the second wife of Elkana, an Ephrathite (meaning a citizen of Bethlehem which is significant to what we are about to share), was barren and had no children because the Lord had shut her womb. In desperation she pleaded before the Lord in the temple, attended by Eli the High Priest in Shiloh, that she would dedicate her first born to the Lord, thus following the law of the Nazarite. She unknowingly fulfilled in her body the law of the first-born given to Moses (1 Samuel 1:1-28). Her first born, Samuel, became a powerful prophet to the kings of Israel.

Who else do we know who fulfilled this law? Father God. He chose Mary the mother of Yeshua to dedicate her first born to the Lord. Joseph was not to know her until after Yeshua's birth. Yeshua, the eternal Spirit known in eternity as the Word (John Chapter 1), became the first-born of God by his incarnation in the flesh through the holy seed delivered to Mary. Jesus was therefore consecrated according to the Law of Moses and was holy to the Lord well before his water baptism.

Father God dedicated his first-born (in human flesh) to save the world and offered him as a sacrifice, not by the blood of bulls as in the case of the Levitical rituals, but by his own blood from Gethsemane to the cross. He was the Lamb of God, "*Agnus Dei.*" At the Feast of Passover, Yeshua was sacrificed according to the Law and became the first fruit of many to come. In speaking to the Gentiles the apostle Paul wrote, "*For if the firstfruit be holy, the lump is also holy: and if the root be holy, so are the branches*" (Romans 11:16). He was referring to Christ, where in 1 Corinthians 15:20 Paul mentions Christ as the "*first fruits of those* who have fallen asleep." What an assurance for us! If Jesus was made holy at birth then so are we at our new birth when we become a new creation. Of course, we can always walk away from what we were given (Hebrews 6:4-8).

"*Passover falls at the time of the beginning of the spring harvest. Leviticus 23:10–16 discusses the omer [a certain measure] of new barley that was brought to the Temple on the second day of the festival. At this time of year, the first sheaf of newly cut barley was offered up as a sacrifice.... The Temple was the focal point for the "shalosh regalim,"* [the three major] *Pilgrim Festivals, and it provided a place for carrying out the Pesach sacrifice*" (My Jewish Learning website).

First Fruits is part of the appointed Feast of Passover when the priests waved a sheaf of the firstfruit of the barley harvest before the Lord in the Temple. This is the Christian principle of us bringing the first fruit of our harvest to the Lord – perhaps our first week's wages or the first profit of our business endeavour.

The pattern for perfection, body ministry within and between Jewish and Gentile Christians was intimated in the previous chapter in relationship to the biblical theme of the 'The Key of David', under the sub-heading Body Ministry: Key of David (2 Chronicles 8:12-16). Satan knows full-well the powerful spiritual synergism that will arise once Messianic Hebrews and Gentile Christians join under the Lord's anointing (Psalm 133, MKJV).

"A Song of degrees; of David. Behold, how good and how pleasant it is for brothers to dwell together in unity! It is like the precious ointment on the head that ran down on the beard, Aaron's beard, that went down to the mouth of his garments; like the dew of Hermon that came down on the mountains of Zion; for there Jehovah commanded the blessing, life forevermore".

The devil is not ignorant. People who revere the Lord more deeply than others in obedience threaten his desires to become like God (Lucifer's five 'I wills' in Isaiah 14:12-15). Lucifer means light bearer which is why he can blind so many Christians. *"So says Jehovah of Hosts: In those days ten men, out of all languages of the nations, shall take hold, and will seize the skirt of a man, a Jew, saying, we will go with you, for we have heard that God is with you"*, (Zechariah 8:23, MKJV).

Idols and Betrayals

Strong personalities and charismatic speakers can become idols. We have seen many high-profile TV personalities, and their wealthy organizations fall in recent years. Some claimed that its payback time for God to give them wealth for all they have done. It seems that despite their early faithfulness and wonderful presentations and prestigious study books on the Bible, they became empire builders towards the end to satisfy their personal passions; not unlike King Solomon who angered God towards the end of his lifetime. It is interesting that at the height of his wealth Solomon received 666 talents of gold in tribute annually, about US$940,000 a very handsome income. 666 is prophetic of something fearful (Revelation 13:18). Solomon became unpopular towards the end of his 40-year reign because he raised taxes when he already had more than sufficient.

"Rehoboam went to Shechem, where all the people of northern Israel had gathered to make him king. When Jeroboam son of Nebat, who had gone to Egypt to escape from King Solomon, heard this news, he returned from Egypt. The people of the northern tribes sent for him, and then they all went together to Rehoboam and said to

him, "Your father Solomon treated us harshly and placed heavy burdens on us. If you make these burdens lighter and make life easier for us, we will be your loyal subjects" (1 Kings 12:1-4). Rehoboam decided to make their lives even harder, so Israel split into two kingdoms because of the King's and his young counsellors' greed.

In the early years of Billy Graham, a preacher by name of Charles Templeton was considered to be the best evangelist in the USA. He took Billy with him to Auschwitz to look at the former death camp before their crusade in Russia. Upon deep reflection Charles said to Billy, *"We are serving the wrong God. A loving God would never have allowed the Jews to suffer so much."* Billy was almost swayed away from Jesus. One night he intensely sought God's face in his garden. The only word from God was, *"Have faith."* He was given no explanation nor Bible verse. Close to death, despite swaying momentarily on TV from Jesus being the only way to salvation, Billy confessed that he was a sinner and asked God for forgiveness. In his lifetime Billy never claimed to know or understand the whole of Scripture, as he would say at some of his crusades to comfort the crowds who didn't understand them either. On the other hand, in 1996 Charles Templeton published his book *Farewell to God: My reasons for rejecting the Christian faith"* which stunned evangelical America. He died an atheist in hospital in 2001 with words to the effect, *"I still love Jesus. What a pity that he wasn't God."*

Some Jewish Messianic worshippers are in danger of not transitioning entirely to the New Testament but continue to hold dearly on to Old Testament traditions of the 'Holy Land' that they are apparently loathed to let go. Some Messianic Christians go to the extreme of firing their pots at Passover not to have leaven in their kitchens missing the spiritual significance of leaven altogether. Others insist on Kosher foods, despite Peter's vison that God has cleansed all animals for food before he went to the house of Cornelius a Gentile. Where will it stop? Will these people re-introduce circumcision which false teachers attempted to do in Jerusalem before the apostle Paul turned up? If those rituals and habits are encouraged to be continued by those weak in the faith, will it become comparable to the blatant idolatry evident in Orthodox Christianity, such as in the Catholic, Egyptian Coptic, Russian, Maltese and Greek churches?

Genuine Gentile churches do not hoard idols, either mental or physical. Charles remembers visiting a

Messianic Church in the USA back in the 1980s. Rabbis took great pride in carrying around an ornate cabinet that held a huge scroll of the Torah (the 'Holy Ark' in Jewish synagogues). It reminded Charles of the Egyptian Coptic church which exhibit all their paraphernalia, icons, flags and 'holy water" in a procession before holding the service. Charles was a special guest of the visiting Coptic Bishop from Egypt and was touched by the Lord when the bishop sprinkled Charles and others with 'holy water' during the service; but how much better would the Word have been without focussing on all those idols that distract during the sermon?

The account of the brazen serpent on a pole in the wilderness (Numbers 21:9) makes a good case about idol worship. When Israel murmured against God the Lord sent poisonous snakes into their tents. Many died, but if they came to Moses and looked at the brass pole they were healed. In the Tabernacle all items of furniture in the Outer Court were made of brass signifying a requirement of repentance before entering the Holy Place. When people obeyed and looked at the pole God accepted their repentance in obeying Moses. Others who wouldn't come died in their sin. Years later the brazen serpent became a detestable idol under shady trees in high places of worship as was their evil custom. Righteous King Hezekiah destroyed the poles, *"For unto those days the children of Israel burnt incense to it: and he called it Nehushtan"* (2 Kings 18:4). *Nehushtan* means an object made of copper. Hezekiah knew that it had become spiritually worthless.

Elaborate crosses and pictures of Jesus can be seen in various churches, homes and as ornaments worn by many. These items fall into the same category as the brazen serpent. They all point to healing and salvation but themselves become objects of worship. Charles knew a dear catholic family who had a large picture of Jesus above the doorway leading to the lounge room. Could Charles ever entice them to talk about salvation or the work of Jesus? Never.

Charles had a catholic charismatic friend whose family had turned to Ananda Marga, a powerful Hindu sect where they served as associate priests. He prayed a lot for his family and could feel demons coming into the house every night. What did he do? He purchased many small crosses and put one on every windowsill with prayer to prevent the demons from coming in. His family never converted to Christianity and his faith eventually faltered. Do demons only come through open doors and windows?

The message of the merging of Jewish and Gentile Christians has already been enacted in some quarters. However, much more needs to be done to break down the barriers. We can expect this to FastTrack as the Lord's coming approaches ever closer. The worship and other videos coming from Messianic sources has lifted our own worship to new heights. We used *"Dance with Me O Lover of my Soul"* performed by the Paul Wilbur group at our wedding. Other powerful Messianic teachings such as those from Sid Roth and Rabbi Schneider for example, are gaining more and more viewers. What a blessing the Lord is imparting upon his children, both Jew and Gentile.

There is also a downside, however. The subliminal messages that come through from some Israeli worship groups and hosts reveal a sense of superiority of the Messianic Jew over evangelical Christians. The very terms "Messianic and Yeshua" and the general avoidance of "Christian and Jesus" carries the same message. It's important to respect Jewish values for Jesus was a Jew. The apostle Paul, however, a hard and fast devout Benjamite, insisted that Jews and Gentiles are one in Christ. He did not consider one superior to the other, despite all the futuristic prophecies involving the city of Jerusalem.

A further downside of the Messianic movement is their rejection of Christmas simply because it wasn't an Old Testament feast. Christmas has held the Gentiles together for 2000 years. It is a wonderful time of the year that brings warmth and joy into the family home as much as Passover brings the same into Jewish homes. The insistence by Messianic Jewry to rename Easter as Resurrection Day is another deliberate ploy to create a wall of separation between themselves and Gentile Christianity. These attitudes of superiority by Messianic Jewry have created two Christian camps worldwide as serious as the day when Israel split into two entities. Shame on the Messianic movement. If the apostle Paul lived today, he would challenge Messianic Jewry with the words "*is Christ divided?*" and then thrust himself into a long sermon on schisms in the body of Christ which he accused the Corinthian church to be guilty of.

We can imagine Paul giving a modern rendition of 1 Corinthians 3:4 and 3:9, "*One says I am a Messianic Jew while another says I am a Christian. Are you not carnal? Are we not labourers together in Christ to build up the body of Christ?"* While this attitude persists there can be no bride of Christ which so many Messianic worship groups elevate in their lyrics!

A Great Harvest to Come

The prophetic end-of year summer harvest during the Feast of Tabernacles is coming to the world very soon (Isaiah 43:19) — The great world-wide ingathering promised (Exodus 23:34). The Feast of Tabernacles is celebrated in the 7th and last month of the ecclesiastic calendar of the Hebrews. This Feast is prophetic of a great harvest to come in our time. This third mandatory Feast of the Lord had three components:

- **Blowing of Trumpets** — Call to repentance, prayer and self-examination
- **The Day of Atonement** — Perfection of Israel through the blood of a Lamb
- **Booths/Sukkoth** — Rejoicing and feasting on the end-of year harvest
- There was an 8th day after the 7 days that were spent in decorated booths

The prophetic significance of these Feasts for us today are:

1. **The blowing of Trumpets** — Alarm warnings of end time. This started largely with Billy Graham and has continued since with ample warnings that end-time was around the corner. God's last call to unbelievers.
2. **The Day of Atonement** — Perfection and marriage of the bride of Christ. Going out to reap the last harvest.
3. **Booths** — Celebrating the final and greatest harvest in God's timetable.
4. The 8th day is Bible code for a new beginning in a cleansed world (8 on Noah's Ark).

Select Scriptures for the perfected bride's function before the return of Christ are:

"*Let us be glad with delight, and let us give glory to him: because the time is come for the Lamb to be married, and his wife has made herself ready*" (Revelation 19:7, BBE).

"*The Spirit and the bride say, 'Come'. Everyone who hears this should say, 'Come!' If you are thirsty, come! If*

you want life-giving water, come and take it. It's free!"
(Revelation 22:17, CEV).

During the 7-day Feast of Booths in the 7th month, obedient orthodox Jews prayerfully gather summer fruits and boughs of leafy trees and remain in decorated booths to feast and rejoice unto the Lord (Deuteronomy 16:13). These temporary shelters built on roofs or in backyards can be seen during the feast in Jerusalem. Once again, we remind the reader that any event tagged with the number seven is a signpost that the subject matter is relevant to end times.

What is the one-day new beginning (the 8th day at the end of Booths) that shall come at the end of the world? It is the 1000-year Millennium in the presence of Christ when there shall be no tears nor sorrow, nor sickness, etc. (Revelation 20:4). The 1000-year Millennium is equivalent to one prophetic day as already mentioned in Chapter 3 (Psalm 90:4; 2 Peter 3:8). Psalm 84:10 intimates the same, where the psalmist says that one day in the Lord's heavenly court is better than 1000 years spent with the wicked on Earth. Jesus confirmed the principle of the one prophetic day for 1000 years in Luke 13:32 where he

lumped the 2000-year church age together with the 1000-year Millennium forming three of God's days, referring to the overall time span as "*today, tomorrow and the third day*".

"For the Earth shall be filled with the knowledge of the glory of the Lord (JHVH), as the waters cover the sea"
Habakkuk 2:17

Question 1

- Have you been burnt or hurt by a particular church or pastor in the past? Remind yourself of the consequences!
- How did you respond? A. By changing churches? B. By leaving the church? C. By blaming God?
- What help did you seek, if any? Be honest to yourself.
- Are you still bitter about the person or persons?
- What does the Lord's Prayer have to say about your own experience (Luke 11:1-4)?

- Then consider Mark 11:25-26 and what Jesus said about the kingdom of God in Matthew 18:23-35.
- Jot down the reasons why it would be difficult for you to do likewise. What would be the consequences?

Question 2

- Are you a person who genuinely seeks to develop a relationship with the Lord?
- What is your approach to achieve that?
- What was Gloria's approach described in this book?

Question 3

- Have you ever had strange encounters which you couldn't explain?
- Did you ask God in prayer what that was about?
- Do you expect God to provide you with an answer?
- If you did, list the ways in which answers have come to you in the past.
- Write a summary on one or more event/s that you can't get out of your mind.
- Did you learn anything from them? Think about the main lessons learnt. Have you applied them since?

CHAPTER 7

The Bride of Christ

" *Now the natural man does not receive the things from the Spirit of God—to him they are nonsense! Moreover, he is unable to grasp them because they are evaluated through the Spirit*". (1 Corinthians 2:14, CJB).

When Jesus and the apostles ministered to the crowds, it was always according to the principle: first the natural then the spiritual. This is why Jesus used parables from the common, everyday experiences of the Hebrews 2000 years ago. He was especially fond of agricultural messages because nobody could possibly mistake the message, yet they refused to understand. The Rabbis were always the first to understand and were greatly offended when they realized that Jesus was talking about them! Jesus was patient with his own disciples because often they didn't know what Jesus was talking about either.

Jesus was both human and divine – Divine Spirit incarnated in human flesh. The humanity part of him became frustrated at times because he thought that his message was simple enough for anyone to understand. He only explained their spiritual meaning to those who had an ear to hear; he reserved his explanations to his disciples. We shall proceed in a similar way.

As any professional fisherman knows, a boat dragging a net scoops up both good and bad fish. When the catch is brought onto the deck, the bad fish are thrown overboard. Jesus used this analogy to describe what happens spiritually when people of all sorts clamour to enter the kingdom of God. Though they may be attending "church" their heart is far from God. In this parable the net is the word of the gospel, the fish are those brought in through the gospel, while the fishermen are faithful disciples preaching the gospel. The sea represents a multitude of people — the world, "*The waters which you saw, where the harlot sits, are peoples and multitudes and nations and tongues,*" (Revelation 17:15).

"*Once more, the Kingdom of Heaven is like a net thrown into the lake, that caught all kinds of fish. When it was full, the fishermen brought the net up onto the shore, sat down and collected the good fish in baskets, but threw the bad fish away. So it will be at the close of the age — the angels will go forth and separate the evil people from among the righteous and throw them into the fiery furnace, where they will wail and grind their teeth,*" (Matthew 13:47–50, CJB).

Regular church attendees will surely have noticed that there are diverse congregations and that there are diverse people in congregations, some very edifying and some downright negative, even rude. Jesus said that there will always be tares in the church. Tares are a wild look-alike wheat that may infest wheat fields. They look identical and cannot be distinguished from wheat until the final harvest, and they often carry disease. It is likely that it was rye weed infesting wheat crops that Jesus was talking about. Rye can carry a deadly dark fungus called *Ergot* which has been known to poison and incapacitate hundreds to a few thousand people dating from the Roman period to the Middle-Ages when it wasn't separated before making flour. Poisonings occurred through bread making and beer production. Anyone who associates with people by continually forgiving and pitying them on a regular basis but who never seem to learn, then the apostle Paul would have a word for you, "*Do not be misled: 'Bad company corrupts good character'*" (1 Corinthians 15.33, NIV).

Yeshua put before them another parable. "*The Kingdom of Heaven is like a man who sowed good seed in his field; but while people were sleeping, his enemy came and sowed weeds among the wheat, then went away. When the wheat sprouted and formed heads of grain, the weeds also appeared. The owner's servants came to him and said, 'Sir didn't you sow good seed in your field? Where have the weeds come from?' He answered, 'An enemy has done this.' The servants asked him, 'Then do you want us to go and pull them up?' But he said, 'No, because if you pull up the weeds, you might uproot some of the wheat at the same time. Let them both grow together until the harvest; and at harvest-time I will tell the reapers to collect the weeds first and tie them in bundles to be burned, but to gather the wheat into my barn'"* (Matthew 13:24–30, CJB).

Our point is this: The kingdom of God on earth is the church or the body, loosely so called. It has in it both good and bad fish; only in rare instances are we able to judge who is who—we cannot judge, only the Lord knows those who are His. However, the Lord can ring alarm bells in our spirit who not to befriend.

The church is not the bride of Christ, but the reverse is true: The bride will emerge out of the church as the five-fold ministries mentioned in Ephesians 4:11-13 perfect responsive individuals. Note that the task of the five-fold ministry Apostle, Prophet, Pastor, Teacher, and Evangelist is not to do the work themselves but to equip us and to bring teachable Christians alongside so that they too can mature further in Christ – to the eventual fulness of peoples to the fullness and stature of Christ. Hard to imagine, isn't it?

That is what we mean by "walking or being processed towards perfection"— not once we get to heaven but right here on planet Earth before the resurrection. Read these verses again prayerfully. The word 'until' is crucial — the five-fold ministry will not cease to exist until the bride is perfected on the Earth. Once she is perfected the bride has a ministry on Earth to gather in the final harvest with an evangelistic message. We recommend that Revelation Chapters 21 and 22 be read slowly and prayerfully, especially Revelation 22:17.

Some churches have stated in their constitutions that the five-fold ministries and several of the nine spiritual gifts no longer exist, so they only have pastors. What a blunder if you have to live with that as a pastor, being only one of the five!

Regarding the necessity for perfection of the bride, let's face it, why would Christ contemplate on being wed to a bride who is not righteous, weaker though she will be? Consider the following demanding requirements:

"That He might present it to Himself as the glorious church, without spot or wrinkle or any such things, but that it should be holy and without blemish" (Ephesians 5:27, MKJV).

"In the body of His flesh through death, to present you holy and without blemish, and without charge in His sight" (Colossians 1:22, MKJV).

"But with the precious blood of Christ, as of a lamb without blemish and without spot" (1 Peter 1:19. MKJV).

"Therefore, beloved, looking for these things, be diligent, spotless, and without blemish, to be found by Him in peace" (2 Peter 3:14, MKJV).

"Now to Him being able to keep you without stumbling, and to set you before His glory without blemish, with unspeakable joy" (Jude 1:24, MKJV).

"And in their mouth was found no guile, for they were without blemish before the throne of God" (Revelation 14:5, MKJV).

The requirement is holy behaviour and actions. The forgiveness of sins cannot accomplish that, but the slow process of maturing in Christ, if one remains teachable, will. The entire Bible, from Genesis to Revelation is a progressive account of the Father's patient work to create a bride for the Son who was ordained from before the beginning, *"And all dwelling on the earth will worship it, those whose names have not been written in the Book of Life of the Lamb slain, from the foundation of the world"* (Revelation 13:8, MKJV).

The book of Revelation is and can be terrifying. It's an account of disasters that God will bring upon unbelievers towards the end of the world, but its hidden purpose is to edify Christians who are looking forward to their final redemption and perfection through the resurrection (Luke 21:1). There is a continuous thread on the theme of the bride of Christ from Revelation Chapter 1 through to the end of the book. Most YouTube presentations concentrate on End Time prophecies to inform us what's going to happen next. While that will bring many to Christ, our desire is for Christians to aim higher towards the perfection promised in Ephesian 4:11-13. We wish to awaken Christians to ready themselves to become members of the bride of Christ.

CHARLES & GLORIA JORIM PALLAGHY

The book of Revelation reveals much about the bride of Christ and, if read carefully, tells us that she will evangelize the world before the Antichrist, together with the false prophet, are revealed and recognized by all. The Antichrist, Satan fully possessing a man, will desire to rule over the world from his throne in the third Temple (surely to be built) in Jerusalem calling himself God (2 Thessalonians 2:4): The worldly one government under the Antichrist is on the horizon. The world will be given a final opportunity to respond to an anointed word from the perfected bride, a multitude sold out to Christ even unto death.

"The Spirit and the Bride say, 'Come!' Let anyone who hears say, 'Come!' And let anyone who is thirsty come—let anyone who wishes, take the water of life free of charge" (Revelation 22:17, MKJV).

Many Bible teachers misinterpret the first part of this verse. They teach that the bride is calling to Jesus wanting the Second Coming to hurry up. But, reading on, why would she call Jesus to come as though he is thirsty for the truth? It's incredible that any church should be found teaching such rubbish.

"Now we beseech you, my brothers, with regard to the coming of our Lord Jesus Christ and our gathering together to Him, that you should not be soon shaken in mind or troubled, neither by spirit, nor by word or letter, as through us, as if the Day of Christ is at hand. Let not anyone deceive you by any means. For that Day shall not come unless there first comes a falling away, and the man of sin shall be revealed, the son of perdition, who opposes and exalts himself above all that is called God, or that is worshiped, so that he sits as God in the temple of God, setting himself forth, that he is God. Do you not remember that I told you these things when I was still with you? And now you know what holds back, for him to be revealed in his own time. For the mystery of lawlessness is already working, only he is now holding back until it comes out of the midst. And then the lawless one will be revealed, whom the Lord shall consume with the breath of His mouth and shall destroy with the brightness of His coming, whose coming is according to the working of Satan with all power and signs and lying wonders, and with all deceit of unrighteousness in those who perish, because they did not receive the love of the truth, so that they might be saved. And for this cause God shall send them strong delusion, that they should believe a lie, so that all those who do not believe the truth, but delight in

unrighteousness, might be condemned" (2 Thessalonians 2:1–12, MKJV).

What Hinders the Bride of Christ from Gaining Perfection?

"For rebellion is as the sin of witchcraft and stubbornness as is iniquity and idolatry."

1 Samuel 15:23 (CJB)

The tragic outcome of Cain who brought an unacceptable burnt offering to the Lord is perhaps the best expression of rebellion and pride in the Bible. Cain brought the sweat of his labours to the altar, the best of fruits and vegetables he had grown. God rejected his offering but accepted that of his brother Abel who brought a lamb. Whether taught to him by his parents Adam and Eve, or whether it came by revelation to Abel is immaterial. A sacrificial lamb foreshadowed Christ's blood shed on the cross. Abel's offering was by faith (Hebrews 11:4), whereas Cain brought works of the flesh to the altar. The brothers illustrated the difference between the two covenants – 'Works under the Law 'and 'Grace by Faith'. Grace by Faith supersedes the old covenant by far which false teachers attempt to revive even in our day.

Levitical priests serving in the tabernacle were never to wear woollen garments because they would become sweaty signifying works of the flesh instead of grace. Works were prohibited in God's Tabernacle. The Law was a schoolmaster (Galatians 3:24-25). The Law taught them that the remission of sin could only be attained by the shedding of blood (Hebrews 9:22). God's grace is freely offered to all who believe, it is not attained by works of our flesh.

To be true to the title of our book I must lay bare what hinders us from fully following Christ by using our marriage relationship to prove a point. I suspect that the matter I am going to raise is common to most of us. Although I never thought of myself as being rebellious, the Lord revealed in recent weeks that the sin of rebellion lurks in the hidden recesses of my soul. It only needs a trigger to be expressed through the way I behave.

I have always been dismayed by ministers of the gospel who refuse correction. For example, regarding the interpretation of a verse that is blatantly incorrect.

A pastor proud of having spent years in bible school, insisted one day that the giants of old were as tall as Cedar trees. He was mortified that I couldn't agree with him. I said to him over dinner that according to the scriptures even Goliath was only about 9 feet tall. He would have been a giant in David's eyes. I challenged the pastor, *"You are surely referring to Behemoth, a dinosaur, which had a tail as large as a Cedar tree"* (Job 40:25-24). He stubbornly insisted in front of his wife that it was I who was mistaken. Finally, I suggested that we could settle the matter by looking up the verse in Job. He became even more defiant, "Men were as tall as cedar trees". *"Can you hand me your Bible? It will only take us three minutes that it refers to an ancient dinosaur whom Job was acquainted with and fearful of."* As soon as I said that he stormed out of the room and went to bed. That was the beginning to the end of our relationship.

In his mind he was referring to Amos 2:9 where the awesome power of the Amorites was likened to "cedar trees with roots" as a metaphor. The prophet was not referring to the literal height of the Amorites "whose height was as tall as cedars". This type of metaphor was used frequently of powerful nations in Judges 9:6-21 for example.

I always thought of myself as being a teachable person, until I found myself in the daily company of my new wife from Papua New Guinea. We had cultural problems almost from the first couple of days when we met in Australia. I could come to terms with them after a while, but what really got under my skin is when we quibbled about what I thought were trivial matters. In my first marriage we addressed each other by our pen names believing that terms like honey and darling were too ingratiating, meaning too sweet, intending to get approval or favour. I was simply Kali and she was Mili, for the entire for 57 years.

However, whenever I called my second wife by her name, her face would become angry. "*Call me honey or darling, but never use my name, especially not in public. Referring to me by my name is disrespectful and unloving.*" I felt like a school kid being told off by a headmistress. It spoiled my mood. Even though we live in Australia I would have to call her Australian brother-in-law Papa, instead of using his name because his wife was her older sister. This sort of thing irked me for weeks. Any younger woman close to her was her 'daughter', making me wonder how many children she had that I had never been told about. My response was to feel inadequate and that she should have married someone else. I hit back by giving her the silent treatment, followed up with an occasional unkind word intended to hurt her. Gloria couldn't understand why I reacted that way. Thank the Lord that that is behind us!

Her devotion to Christ is impeccable. She taught me much about holiness, but I continued to resent matters she brought up because I thought them trivial. Major corrections I have no problems with; it's the little things that seem to put up a barrier between the two of us at times, which made me think of a verse in Song of Songs (2:15, CJB),

"Catch the foxes for us – yes, the little foxes that spoil our vineyard when the vineyard is in bloom."

In this way the Lord brought my own sin of rebellion towards His Word to my attention, the little things in life that prevent me from going on unto perfection. I confess that I began to take on a seed of Cain's tragic attitude; to sulk and be tempted to walk away from relationship (Genesis 4:10-16, Hebrews 11:4; Jude 1:11).

I prayed about it and became convicted that I should write about it perchance it's the little things in life that prevent the bride from reaching her promised state of perfection. We don't need a new revelation or a complex theology concerning the bride of Christ. For the bride of Christ to be totally without blemish, as the apostle Paul put it in Ephesians 5:27, is a high calling that most of us find impossible to believe. That is why the subject of 'perfection' is never taught in church because we know the deepest of our own failings and are reluctant to repent. Yet, absolute perfection in our flesh shall be fulfilled prior to the Second Coming as a careful reading of Ephesians 4:11-13 will confirm.

This, I believe, is a challenge facing church leaderships because judgment must first begin in the house of God (1 Peter 4:17). Little, seemingly insignificant, things are the cause of primary divides. Rarely does one hear a pastor apologize from the pulpit when he/she becomes aware of their error. Do I tremble by daring to put this in our book? Of course I do, but I believe that in the long run the truth shall set us free no matter what.

The New Jerusalem: The City of God

The book of Revelation describes the city of the New Jerusalem as a huge cube, with its sides as long as the breadth of Australia. Note that it is a city within the vast expanses of Paradise (Revelation 20:9). Though the description is symbolic, it is not symbolic at the same time because the description contains some realities. It is too wonderful to describe. The closest we can come to it is by considering an analogy; have you ever given thought to the strange planet we are living on? Firstly, the only solid thing about the Earth is the outer core which is very shallow in some places of high volcanic activity allowing the liquid magma (lava) to squirt out in erruptions. We are sitting on the surface of a ball of red-hot liquid, protected from burning to ashes by the thin outer core.

In deep Outer Space galaxies are receding from each other at unimaginable speeds. We are swept along as passengers on spaceship Earth which itself is only a passenger too. In our own galaxy there are suns up to 1500 times the size of our own sun. If the rotation of the Earth around its own axis were to suddenly stop, we and anything else not fixed to the earth's outer core, would be flung into Outer Space together with all the oceans and all the molten magma (lava) from volcanoes. The Earth would be torn apart! Spaceship Earth is a very strange place to live on indeed.

Next consider jet travel around the Earth. Within only a matter of hours we are walking upside down relative to where we were only half a day earlier. Do we think about it when we arrive at distant airports? No, we don't. We get off the aircraft and walk normally, up being up and down being down, but relative to where we were up is down and down is up. Not for a moment do we think about it, do we? It is our norm. If we were to consider our families back home, they are walking upside down relative to us in our new location. When we make a phone call, we don't think of them as being upside down, do we? We imagine them to be as up as we are, relative to the earth's surface. If the phone were handed to one of our children and he or she trips and falls down we don't think of them as having fallen up, do we? Yet relative to us, they have fallen up!

To make our existence even more strange let's consider Earth time. Atomic clocks have proven that time is relative to gravity. Time runs at a different rates on the top of Mount Everest as compared to a clock at sea level. Time is different on the surface of Jupiter compared to us because it is so much heavier than the Earth. In far flung solar systems where their suns might be hundreds of times heavier than our Sun, their time will be running at very different rate relative to us. Thousands or billions of years might have passed there within a year of our time. At the speed of light time ceases altogether as the Jew, Albert Einstein, and scientific experimentation have proven. If we were to approach the speed of light, the time dilation between us relative to those back on earth would approach infinity. Check it out with Dr. Google.

Now consider the Bible itself. Jesus called himself the light of the world. Adonai's temples always had to face directly East towards the rising Sun (Numbers 2:3; 10:5). In the days of Moses, the number of men capable of military service camped to the East of the door of the Tabernacle facing the rising Sun was 186,400 (Numbers Chapters 2 and 3). This number happens to match very closely the speed of light in miles per second today (which some physicists have claimed has decayed ever so slowly since the days of Moses, despite it being considered a universal constant, thus perhaps matching it exactly when Moses was alive. This is a sign from God that He is in charge of all things.

Note that the three tribes camped to the East, Judah, Issachar and Zebulon, were called the camp of Judah. They led the Hebrews through the wilderness under the banner of a lion (Genesis 49:9-10; Revelation 5:5) which they considered an honour. The other tribes marched behind them under their own banners. The Exodus was not a rabble fleeing from Egypt. (This camp of Judah must not to be confused with Judah at the head of the southern kingdom, after united Israel was split, which was comprised of the tribes Judah, Benjamin and Levi – the Jews or Judahites).

In space crafts, the difference in time between it and Mission Control on earth is tiny but must be accounted for by the computers to time rocket burns at precise moments not to irreversibly fling the craft into deep space.

God has clearly indicated that a 24-hour day is different to the length of a day where He is located in heaven (Psalms 84:10; 90:4; 2 Peter 3:8. See also End Times: According to Scripture by Charles Pallaghy, Bookside Press, 2023). In Luke 13:32 Jesus referred to the 2000-year church age and the 1000-year millennium as "*Today, tomorrow and the third day*". We just didn't want to or don't want to believe it, because it's too strange a concept.

In declaring creation by the spoken word in Genesis Chapters 1 and 2, God obviously measures time according to the length of time where He was located then, not according to a 24-hour day on the earth. It is important to bear in mind that years and days did not exist until Day 4 of the creation when God created the Solar System. In addition, the length of a day differs between planets according to their speed of rotation because of differences in gravity and composition. Time is relative, not an absolute, as experiments based on Albert Einstein's theories have proven.

Having hopefully realised the peculiarities of our planet we can move on to consider the strangeness of heaven relative to where we are now. The bride city of the New Jerusalem is described as a huge cube (Revelation 21:9-27), whose foundation is based on the names of the 12 apostles. A description impossible to justify to our minds. What is God trying to tell us mere humans? What is the mystery God has set before us? Yeshua told the apostle John to write it down and that anyone who keeps the prophecies of the book of Revelation will be blessed. Revelation repeats this promise seven times. However, there is also a stern warning that anyone who adds to or subtracts from the words of the prophesy will pay the ultimate penalty. Therefore, let us tread very carefully here. None of us wish to end up in the Lake of Fire. We shall only touch the surface of the subject because it is too wonderful. Apart from a few seed thoughts presented here, Charles may elaborate a little more on the subject provided the Lord so directs him in his forthcoming book, '*Immortal to the End: A Challenging True Story of the Supernatural*', Bookside Press, 2024.

What else do we know about the New Jerusalem, the bride city? It is semi-symbolically a huge cube because of the presence of the Lord, as the lord foreshadowed by the Most Holy Place in the Temple being cubic in measure. It involves the names of the 12 apostles and the twelve tribes of Israel. The huge cube therefore also represents people, numerous in number. It is bejewelled and glows with the glory of God having no need for a Sun, because the Lamb is the light of it. It has no Temple because the Lord Himself is its Temple. It is a river of life according to prophecies and is totally holy, free of sickness and sin. It is full of joy. The cross and the blood of the Lamb is at its centre. In addition, Yeshua said that He is preparing a room or mansion for each one of us. According to a vision or dream Charles had on his brief visitation to heaven, our homes seem to be mansions. What can we make of all that?

It is a place of righteousness and worship where we all have access to the King of a multitude of the redeemed, yet He will treat each one of us intimately as individuals, all at the same time. In heaven there will be no concept of linear time as we have here on the earth, the presence of the Lord is simultaneously everywhere. We already know that on earth, don't we? The Holy Spirit hears the prayer of a submariner deep underneath the surface of the ocean as much as he hears every believer around the planet, all at the same time! The only analogy on earth that comes close to the attributes of God is a super-fast computer on the internet that can handle thousands of bits of information sent in by different people from all over the globe, all at the same time.

The New Jerusalem has a high wall. Cities have walls to indicate a separation and security inside as compared to those living outside (in Paradise, for those not in the bride). There are 12 gates guarded by angels on all sides indicating accessibility to all fulfilling preset conditions. The number 12 is embedded in its description, twelve being a number of authority tagging those inside, the shape indicative of equality as viewed from anywhere outside. Regarding its physical size, a city of that size could comfortably hold a collective of billions of select redeemed people from all eras of world history.

In addition, we are all in Him, as numerous scriptures in the New Testament declare. The mystery deepens the more one thinks about it, but we can be assured that all of the above apply to those inside the city. It is a perfect geometric figure symbolising the perfection of the Lord whose presence dwells in the midst of His people, Emmanuel – its variant Immanuel meaning *"God with us or amongst us"*. It is a masculine name derived from the Hebrew, verifying that though the city is a bride it is also the abode of the sons of God. Amongst the Hebrews, males were heads and the authority of households, while in the New Testament the number 12 also denotes the authority of scripture such as the apostolic or unadulterated doctrine of the twelve. Usage of 'sons of God' can include humans of both genders, for example when God referred to all the Hebrews in Goshen, male and female, as my *"firstborn son"* (Exodus 4: 21-23). Pray and mull over what we have given you and see what the Lord reveals to you personally. Jesus said that the person of the Holy Spirit will lead us into all truth. These seed thoughts are all we can mention without stepping outside of the Word of God.

The Antichrist

The Antichrist can be best understood by considering his prototype, Judas Iscariot who betrayed Yeshua with a kiss. Judas had been planning for a long time to do exactly that and the Father foretold Jesus that he had a devil amongst the twelve. Judas was apparently a zealot for Israel wanting to rid the people from foreign rule. Once he realized that Jesus had no such intention his soul began brewing sin to the point where Satan was able to enter his heart as Jesus gave him communion (Luke 22:3; John 13:27). Paul warned never to take communion with sin in our heart lest it become detrimental instead of a blessing,

"So that whoever shall eat this bread and drink this cup of the Lord unworthily, he will be guilty of the body and blood of the Lord. But let a man examine himself, and so let him eat of that bread and drink of that cup. For he who

eats and drinks unworthily eats and drinks condemnation to himself, not discerning the Lord's body. For this cause many among you are weak and sickly, and many sleep" (1 Corinthians 11:27-30).

Another thing we learn about Judas is that he was the apostles' treasurer. He helped himself secretly from the common purse (John 12:6) because, as Jesus said, Judas was a thief. What can we surmise from this to be true to the pattern set by Judas?

Here are some key thoughts about the Antichrist: If Judas is a prototype, then he shall probably have a form of religion. He will make a show of participating in communion but deny Christ. He will be interested in economics pretending it to be advantageous for people; He will command respect because of the company he keeps and, finally, he will probably be interested in economics to enrich himself. 666 spells perfection in worldly ways, since 6 is the number of man, signifying ultimate power of the flesh. Everything about Goliath was measured in 6's. When King Solomon became greedy, he was receiving 666 talents of gold in tribute in gold from other nations.

Question

- Jesus came to preach that the kingdom of God has come. What did Jesus say about those who responded to his message? Summarise the lessons you discover by reading Matthew 13:24-30 and 47-50.
- Has this shocked you or have you heard this preached before?
- Would you comfortably equate the kingdom of God on Earth with the current church (think of the church as the combination of all Christian denominations around the world)?
- Read the statement of the apostle Paul in Ephesians 5:24-32. Make a column of three with the headings: The church, The body of Christ: The bride of Christ. After listing what you have read about them would you be prepared to equate 'the church' with the 'bride of Christ' as being synonymous?
- Into which category would you currently place yourself?
- Read Revelation chapters 21 and 22. What can be said about the bride of Christ? Is she made ready on Earth or only once Christians are in heaven?

CHAPTER 8

Those Not in the Bride of Christ

Spiritual Symbolism of the Temples

The number 10 is Bible code for a testing or trial. What tests do we have to pass to be included in the bride?

Even as Solomon's Temple, which was permanent, was an upgrade of the Tabernacle of Moses which was mobile, so Solomon's Temple is also an upgrade regarding our spiritual requirements in the kingdom of God; expressed by the massive amount of symbolism it contains in comparison to the simple Tabernacle of Moses. The symbolism of the Tabernacle of Moses is sufficient for entry into God's presence in Paradise. Solomon's Temple, however, has many more stringent requirements to proceed from the Outer Court into the Most Holy Place. This is because it relates to those who aspire to accept the high calling of God to participate in the bride of Christ in the end times. This offer is open to every man, woman and child.

The first thing to note about Solomon's Temple is that it was much bigger in size, yet the Most Holy Place was still cubic indicating God's presence. Secondly, in the equivalent to the Tabernacle Outer Court, we now have 10 lavers for washing instead of one and there is an extra gauntlet, so to speak, that priests had to pass through before they could get to the Holy Place. Remembering that the number 10 is Bible code for a test or testing, it suggests that God is going to inspect the way in which we were baptised much more stringently than for the general redeemed person. In what way you might ask? When Paul met disciples of John the Baptist in Acts Chapter 19, he insisted on rebaptising them into the name of the Lord Jesus Christ, not just into the name of the Father, Son and Holy Spirit, but actually employing the family name (check out how baptism was carried out after the resurrection). He also laid hands on them to receive the Holy Spirit. Receiving the baptism of the Holy Spirit enabled them to pray in tongues and to prophesy. Paul said he delighted praying in tongues when he didn't know what to pray for. It also edifies us, so let's not disrespect the place of tongues in our prayer life.

They were 12 in number and lived in Ephesus. The number 12, the number of authority, suggests that these ones were going to set up the church in Ephesus. Ephesus was the first and most important of the seven churches in the book of Revelation. Thus, the Lord is going to inspect our baptism whether we were only sprinkled, without even first repenting as is the tradition in some churches, and so on. If that describes you, then its time to read Acts chapter 2 and do something about it.

What is the extra gauntlet? Before the Levitical priests could minister in the Holy Place they had to pass by two massive brass columns, Jachin and Boaz, with a circumference of 12 cubits each. The mention of brass means repentance. It would require a Bible study for us to explain it all, but you may wish to look at the book by Charles (End Times: According to Scripture, 2023). The symbolism reveals that God is going to thoroughly scrutinize the genuineness of our repentance by the apostolic word in the times of the end, there being two columns signifying an authority of 12 that was at the beginning of the church age and another authority of 12 towards the end of the church age. Much more could be said in the way the capitals of the columns were symbolically decorated with chains and fruits. We remind our readers that Paul called himself a prisoner of the Lord. Are we really prisoners of the Lord or do we still exercise our free will?

Once inside the Holy Place there were ten tables of showbread offering 12 x 10 loaves of holy bread. The number 120 signifies the end of all flesh: God gave the world 120 years before he destroyed them with a world-wide flood. It is also not coincidence that there were 120 disciples in the upper room when they were filled with the Spirit on the Day of Pentecost. It marked the end of their flesh. Now they were willing to die for their testimony, whilst before they hid behind locked doors for they feared the Levitical Priests and Temple guards.

Instead of one 7-branched candlesticks there are now ten, each placed to illuminate each of the ten tables of showbread separately. The bread, the word of God, was going to be intensely illuminated by the Holy Spirit, much more than ever before. This means that a person's spiritual status who has symbolically followed through from being saved by the blood in the Outer Court must have a superior impartation of God's Word to be eventually counted in the bride. We must proceed to further maturity as the apostle Paul said, by being filled with the Spirit and much more, to proceed beyond the first principles of Christ (Hebrews Chapter 5). A Pentecostal church might think that they have it all, but Paul said that everything that is normally practised there is only a beginning – they are only the first principles of the doctrines of Christ. We need to mature beyond those practices.

If you find this too complex to comprehend, don't worry about it. **RELAX**. We don't wish to throw you off. **God is after our hearts not our knowledge!!!** His Holy Spirit will provide us with all we need by his wonderful grace. We don't need to strive. **All we have to say is *"Yes Lord, please count me in"*.** We can't boast, we can't claim to be better, for God loves the humble, but if we say yes, the Lord will elevate us to his requirements and fill us with his love, towards his own people especially.

The simple message is that the Lord Adonai is going to select those with a pure heart for inclusion in his select bride. His bride must be perfect. If you have a desire to follow the Lord all the way, all that Adonai requires of you is to hand over your will and let him perfect you through the five-fold ministry (Ephesians 4:11-13). Yes, we must be teachable, and it will include both suffering for Christ and much joy, but isn't it worth it? Think how short our life on earth is in comparison to our potential reward now and in eternity.

In the parable of the ten virgins five of them entered through the gate but five missed out. They were short of oil. The five who missed out did not possess enough oil while waiting for the marriage to come to pass (Matthew 25:1-13). All five were virgins meaning that they had been cleansed from sin. Oil represents something about the Holy Spirit. When they knocked on the door pleading to be let in, Jesus said that he didn't know them (Matthew 25:12). It seems that they lost the intimate relationship with the Lord they once had. Relationship is a personal possession the five wise virgins could not give away to their fellow Christians who had obviously neglected their relationship with the Lord (verse 9). Once the marriage takes place it is much too late. According to the Bible the acceptable time is now, indeed this very day.

"Afterward came also the other virgins, saying, Lord, Lord, open to us. But he answered and said, Verily I say unto you, I know you not" (KJV). So, what is it that we must do?

The books of Hebrews and Revelation contain much 'Temple Language' assuming that the reader is well acquainted with the Old Testament. The layout of the Tabernacle of Moses and its various functions described in the books of Exodus and Leviticus illustrate pictorially the progressive pathway in the life an ideal believer should take. As we have mentioned, the Temple of Solomon reveals much more.

Jesus is our forerunner and high priest, *"Yeshua has entered there as a forerunner on our behalf, having become Kohen Gadol "forever, according to the order of Melchizedek."'* (Hebrews 6:20, TLV). Since Jesus is our high priest (Hebrews 5:10) and forerunner, he beckons believers to follow him all the way and to take up our cross. Christ has made us kings and priests through grace (Revelation 1:6; 5:10). It is therefore our privilege to follow in real life what the High Priest had to do symbolically on the Day of Atonement (Yom Kippur) in the Tabernacle of Moses.

Yom Kippur was the only moment in time when Israel was perfected once a year by the 7x sprinkling of the blood of a perfect lamb on the golden Mercy Seat on top of the Ark in the Most Holy Place. Afterwards they quickly resumed sinning once again. The Old Testament ritual performed by the High Priest is a prophetic shadow in symbolic form what Jesus had to accomplish when he offered himself as a living sacrifice to God the Father. It wasn't easy for him. In the Garden of Gethsemane, he sweated blood and wished that he wouldn't have to go through with it, but he submitted himself to the Father. The symbolism of a Christian's walk illustrated through the rituals of the High Priest in the Tabernacle of Moses is unmistakably clear.

Levitical priests, including the High Priest, served the Lord by regularly attending to their required duties inside the Outer Court, the Holy Place and the Most Holy Place. The oil in the lamps had to be refilled (infilling of the Holy Spirit) and the twelve loaves of bread (the word delivered by the apostles) had to be replaced with fresh loaves regularly. The continual burning of incense, on the altar of incense before the vail leading to the Ark of the Covenant, symbolised continual prayer before the Lord. **The symbolism of a Christian's walk illustrated through the rituals of the Tabernacle of Moses is unmistakably clear.**

The tabernacle of Moses is an Old Testament shadow or picture of the pathway by which we are to approach God and be transformed into His image. This is a complex subject needing further study, but we can summarise it simply. It represents in picture form the pathway or series of events which must take place if we are to live in God's presence in eternity. We shall examine this in a moment but let's first appreciate how the gospel was first preached by the New Testament church 2000 years ago. On the Day of Pentecost, an annual celebration of the Jews, the church was born when God poured out His Spirit upon the apostle Peter and others and gave the apostle the following words to preach to the Jews gathered in Jerusalem from distant places, *"Repent from your sins, receive by faith that Jesus shed his blood for the forgiveness of your sins, be renewed and baptised in water, and God will give you the Holy Spirit to dwell in you and to guide you into all truth"*. Fairly simple in essence, don't you think?

On the very Day of Pentecost celebrated in Jerusalem, 3000 Jews were filled with the Holy Spirit and baptised (Acts Chapter 2). The infilling with the Holy Spirit is equivalent to a Levitical priest entering the Holy Place in the Tabernacle where the 7-branched candlestick was the only source of illumination (representing the Holy Spirit in a devotee's life).

The formula given by the apostle Peter on the Day of Pentecost for salvation was brief and to the point. Repentance is the vital ingredient to be acceptable to Christ. However, it is the Tabernacle of Moses that provides the clearest illustration of the stepwise process required for perfection in the Bible.

Passover, the shedding of blood for the forgiveness of sins, is the passport for salvation and for our new birth in Christ. All sacrificial animals whether bulls, sheep, goats or doves were killed before the altar of burnt sacrifice in the Outer Court. All metallic items in the Outer Court were made of brass. For anyone not coming with a repentant heart before God, heaven will be as brass to them (Deuteronomy 28:23); their prayers shall not be heard.

Contemporary Christians might ask the question, "*Why do we need to know about the Tabernacle of Moses and the fact that the Holy Spirit was poured out on a special day of the Jews?*" The simple fact of the matter is that while the New Testament explains much it doesn't explain everything. A New Testament believer will gain much when he begins to understand the steps required towards perfection through both. Symbolism is a powerful tool to bring to one's heart spiritual matters that are virtually impossible to describe in words. It is the lack of such teachings in modern churches that explains why Christian pastors reject the notion of perfection prior to the Second Coming of Christ. Shame on those who do not teach the Old Testament in parallel alongside the New Testament!

We would urge readers to look at important background material presented in a compact form in Charles' book on the end times, along with any other solid material you can find. God will reveal His overall plan and timings by the essential symbolisms hidden in the construction and function of the first (Moses') and second (Solomon's) temples, along with the mandatory Feasts of ancient Israel: Passover, Pentecost and Tabernacles. These are the gaps in the gospels and epistles which we will miss out on unless we put aside time to consider such things.

Maturing in Christ: Shadow of Heavenly Things in the Tabernacle of Moses

We shall present the pathway to perfection illustrated in picture form using the Old Testament as the Lord intended in the first place. We shall trace the stepwise progression of one's necessary development and growth in Christ from being an infant requiring milk to that of a fully mature adult in Jesus Christ.

"For indeed because of the time, you ought to be teachers, you have need that one teach you again what are the first principles of the oracles of God. And you have become in

need of milk, and not of solid food. For everyone partaking of milk is unskillful in the Word of Righteousness, for he is an infant" (Hebrews 5:12-13).

We begin our virtual walk as a worldly sinner by first entering the Tabernacle through the curtain surrounding the Outer Court in the Tabernacle of Moses. Here we meet all the rituals in the Outer Court. We are then allowed to go through the first vail into the Holy Place containing the 7-branched lampstand (representing the fulness of the Holy Spirit), the twelve loaves of bread (representing apostolic doctrine), and the altar of incense (representing prayer). The Holy Place is where the church and Spirit-filled filled individuals are symbolically located spiritually at the present time.

In ancient Israel only the high priest was allowed to enter the Tabernacle from outside the surrounding curtain (representing the world) to proceed right through the vail into the Most Holy Place where the glory of God would speak from between the two golden cherubim on top of the gold-covered wooden Ark of the Covenant.

Then, having met all its requirement, only some individuals are allowed to progress further past the altar of incense (much prayer) through the final veil into the Most Holy Place. The Most Holy Place is where God manifested His Shekinah glory once a year to the High Priest of Israel. Here the High Priest would sprinkle the blood of a lamb 7-times onto the golden Mercy Seat on top of the golden Ark of the Covenant. To protect himself from the holiness of God through much prayer, he had to symbolically take a censor of hot coals with incense. The sweet aroma and cloud prevented him from perishing in the presence of a Holy God.

Progressive Steps of Man: Outer Court Christians

1. The priest lived in a tent outside the Tabernacle. Living outside of God's holy structure represents the unsaved sinner living under his own law of behaviour in the world. Before we are born again, we essentially feed off the Tree of the Knowledge of Good and Evil, as did Adam and Eve, and find it impossible to live a righteous life because of the weakness of our flesh and the lusts we express in different ways

throughout our lives. By entering through the curtain, a priest found himself in the Outer Court where blood was shed for the forgiveness of sin. This is the modern-day equivalent of salvation. However, we mustn't stay in that infantile spiritual state, because of the warning that this may result in a dire outcome in end-times unless he/she moves on: *"And there was given me a reed like unto a rod, and he said unto me, Rise and measure the temple of God and the altar and those that worship therein. But leave out the court which is within the temple and measure it not, for it is given unto the Gentiles, and the holy city shall they tread under foot forty-two months."* (Revelation 11:1-2, JUB).

2. For the forgiveness of sin a person had to bring an offering into the Outer Court where he had to lay his hands on his offering and then slay the innocent animal before a Levitical priest who would carry out the prescribed ritual to cleanse him.

On the Day of Atonement (*Yom Kippur*, once annually) the High Priest entered the Outer Court of the Tabernacle where lamb's blood was shed by the priest; first for himself and then for the nation of Israel. The laver was for the washing of the priest's hands. This ritual foreshadowed Christ pierced on the cross, "*Out came blood and water*". The blood, contaminated by the man's sin, was then poured onto the ground and none of his sins would be remembered by Adonai, the Lord. This is our first step in Christ: Repentance, washings, and the forgiveness of our sins through the blood. We mustn't stay there, otherwise we remain infants in Christ and can only feed on the milk of the word. I.e. Superficial sermons on salvation, gospel stories and the like. We must proceed beyond this to mature in Christ.

After salvation, the next command for a Christian to be fully saved and receive the name of the Lord is to be immersed in water. The Bible commands baptism; it is not an option. The literal meaning in the Greek New Testament of being water baptised is to be immersed in water in the name of the trinity and to die to the temptations of the world. We spiritually arise as a new creation in Christ. Martin Luther got water baptism right when he used the word "*Taufen*" in German, which means "to dive" but somehow the Lutherans lost their way on this matter over the past few centuries (Matthew 28:19). They and some other denominations sprinkle water over both babies and adults. Babies can't repent which is a crucial requirement to be born by the Spirit into the kingdom of God. Haven't pastors read that in the New Testament?

The large laver of water used for washings was in the Outer Court before one entered the Holy Place. Note that baptism is the only way by which to receive the family name of God. However, in our context, that is only a beginning for the infant Christian. According to the preached word by Peter on the Day of Pentecost (Acts chapter 2), Christians need to proceed beyond that and proceed towards maturity.

Forgiveness through the shedding of blood is a mystery that we will never be able to fathom until we are truly in His presence. Let's just accept the living word by faith (Hebrews 11:6, *"For without faith it is impossible to please God"*…And…*"The life of the flesh is in the blood, and that there is no remission of sin without the shedding of* [sinless] *blood"* (Matthew 26:28; Hebrews 9:22). Thus the 'Outer Court' represents the state of a person who refuses to move on but continues to receive the forgiveness of sins and bathes in the warmth of it but does very little with it.

All the vessels in the Outer Court were of burnished, shining brass. Brass is always related to a demand to repent in the Bible. Note how Jesus came with fiery eyes to the churches in Revelation chapters 2 and 3 with burnished feet of brass (Revelation 1:14-15). He didn't like what he saw in six of the seven churches addressed, did He? The number 7 is always related to end times in the Bible and particularly to the book of Revelation, the book of sevens. When we see the number 7 anywhere in the Bible we ought to sit up and take special note.

Spiritual Significance of the Holy Place

3. The High Priest, or serving Levites on normal days, then entered the Holy Place on the Day of Atonement which had a cover of 3 layers (signifying the oversight of the Trinity) hiding it from natural light. The Holy Place represents the 2000-year church age, the *Times of the Gentiles*.

Why? Because it measured 20x10x10 cubits. The curtain surrounding the Outer Court measured 1500 square cubits equivalent to the 1500 years from Moses to the resurrection. The law was given for 1500 years. The church age 2000 years. We are almost there considering that Yeshua was resurrected at about 33 1/2 years after his birth.

The Holy Spirit is given to believers to illuminate the Word of God. The lamp illuminated the 12 fresh loaves of bread on the holy table of shewbread opposite, freshly prepared which signified the doctrine or teachings of the 12 apostles. Jesus referred to himself as *"the bread of life which has come down from heaven"* (John 6:33-51). This becomes the daily bread of believers as they participate in the life of the church assembly.

This is surely clear from Peter's sermon. People are to receive and be filled with the person of the Holy Spirit. Some pastors teach incorrectly that once people are born-again, they are also filled with the

Spirit. They certainly are born of the Spirit, but they may not necessarily be filled with the Spirit! It's one thing to have the Spirit with you, but it's another thing to have the Spirit dwell in you in power. That's why Jesus didn't want the apostles to begin preaching the word, even though Jesus breathed the Holy Spirit upon them before he ascended into heaven. They first had to be filled with power from on high so that they would be able to speak in tongues. The infilling in Acts 2 took place on the very day that the Jewish population was celebrating the Day of Pentecost with their symbolic rituals.

Take the case of Philip the evangelist in Samaria which clearly shows that one can be born again without being filled with the Spirit. Through his preaching people were baptized and many miracles were manifested among the new believers (Acts 8:12–13). That's all well and good, but when the apostles heard that the born-again believers were not filled with the Spirit, they sent Peter and John from Jerusalem to lay hands on them and fill them with the Spirit. The Scripture teaches a two-step process which, depending on the individual, can be separated in time by seconds, days or weeks, or even years or, sadly, never in many cases. Note it was not a case of resistance by a few because the Holy Spirit had fallen upon none of them, despite all the physical miracles.

"And the apostles in Jerusalem hearing that Samaria had received the Word of God, they sent Peter and John to them; who when they had come down, prayed for them that they might receive the Holy Spirit. For as yet He had not fallen on any of them, they were baptized only in the name of the Lord Jesus. Then they laid their hands on them, and they received the Holy Spirit" (Acts 8:14–17).

The Most Holy Place Speaks of Perfection

4. In the Most Holy Place the Shekinah glory of God would shine forth from between the two golden cherubim on top of the mercy seat. In this cubic compartment every metallic object was made of gold to signify the presence of an incorruptible God. 'Shekinah' means *"the manifestation of the presence of God; Divine Presence."*

What was the point of that Mosaic ritual? Why was the blood sprinkled between two Cherubbim? Angels cannot forgive. Two angels acting as a witness were positioned on the golden Mercy Seat to look down on the blood. Below the blood were the two tablets of the Law. Angels cannot charge us for having broken any of the ten, or, all 613 of the Mosaic laws; because of the intervening blood they cannot condemn us. That is why it's called the Mercy Seat.

The Ark also contained an almond rod bearing flowers and fruit and a golden pot of manna. They respectively correspond to the fruitfulness of the Holy Spirit manifested in us and our eating of God's word daily. That's all very well for Israel and today's spirit-filled believers, but what about the verses in Ephesians 4:11-13 that we shall be perfected before the Second Coming? Stay with us and you will find out.

Where Are You in the Order of Things?

In Acts 17:30 the apostle declares, "*Although God overlooked the (our) ignorance of earlier times, He now commands all people everywhere to repent*" (TLV). Since the Second Coming is only a handful of years away it is timely to respond quickly when God calls.

It is significant in the book of Revelation that God tells the angel not to measure or number those who are in the "Outer Court", a reference to their poor spiritual status: That they will be handed over to the Antichrist if they persist to remain in that state without moving on.

*"And a reed like a rod was given to me. And the angel stood, saying, rise up and measure the temple of God, and the altar, and those who worship in it. But leave out the court which is outside the temple, and do not measure it, for it was given to the nations. And they will trample the holy city **forty-two months**"* (Revelation 11:1–2, MKJV).

Note that the Antichrist shall have his rule for three and a half years. Daniel the prophet was given a timeline for the coming of the Messiah by the Archangel Gabriel. This prophecy is so important that the principal demon ruling Persia, current day Iran, fought for 21 days to prevent Gabriel bringing the message to Daniel. Only the intervention of the waring Archangel Michael allowed Gabriel to get through. Gabriel is only the head of messenger angels. We don't realize it but there are angelic wars going on in the heavens unnoticed by the world. The same Prince of Persia is still using his powers to influence Iran to wipe out Israel; angels don't die. It was somehow under God's control that only one third of the angels would rebel. Therefore, the holy angels outnumber the evil ones, we call demons, by two to one. We intimate this because there are two holy Archangels, but only one evil one – Lucifer or Satan.

In Daniel Chapter 9 he was given the 70-week prophecy (spanning 490 years, which is 70 weeks of years) which detailed that Messiah would be cut off in the midst of the week, meaning 3½ years. Jesus ministered for 3½ years after which He was cut off (the time of His baptism to His crucifixion). This was followed by the overspreading of abominations during which time the Jews still practised blood sacrifices (the 2000-year church age)! The remaining half of the week at the end of that will be given to the Antichrist to rule over the world for 3½ years,

*"The beast was allowed to brag and claim to be God, and for **forty-two months** it was allowed to rule. The beast cursed God, and it cursed the name of God. It even cursed the place where God lives, as well as everyone who lives in heaven with God. It was allowed to fight against God's people and defeat them. It was also given authority over the people of every tribe, nation, language, and race. The beast was worshiped by everyone whose name wasn't*

written before the time of creation in the book of the Lamb who was killed" (Revelation 13:5–8, CEV).

Both scriptures refer to the last 42 months or 3 ½ years of the world, the period during which the Holy Spirit is taken from the world, but the bride is protected by God during that time for 1,260 days (3 ½ years) in an unknown place called the wilderness (Revelation 12:6).

'Outer Court Christians' shall die either from starvation or be beheaded if they refuse to take up the mark of the beast (Revelation 20:4). An angel says elsewhere that any who take up the mark of the beast shall have their part in the Lake of Fire together with the devil (Revelation 14:9-10). That's a stern warning for the lukewarm. Devote your life to Jesus while you still can.

Imagine the situation of a father coming home without food for his family because he is not allowed to buy unless he takes on the mark of the beast; nor shall any doctor or hospital look after you. Your young children would be left destitute on the streets to care for themselves as happened to Christians during communism in the Eastern Bloc. "*According to some sources, the total number of Christian victims under the Soviet regime has been estimated to range around 12 to 20 million*" (*Persecution of Christians in the Eastern Bloc*, Wikipedia). That might have also included Jews who had been persecuted in Russia since the communist revolution. Would you want to end up in that situation one day?

Question 1

- Does the content of this chapter shock you?
- Explain the message of the Tabernacle of Moses in your own words. Does it confirm Ephesians 4:11-13 which so many pastors dismiss these days?
- Why do you think we emphasized the merging of Messianic Jews with Gentile Christians? In your answer consider what you might expect to hear from different pulpits.
- Who or what are the Messianic Jews? Take your time and use the content of Chapter 8 to provide the answer in your own words. Use Dr Google if you need help.

Question 2

Jesus specifically commands us to be water baptized in the name of the Father, Son and the Holy Spirit. Why then, in every case when the apostles baptized people after the resurrection, did they not baptise anyone by repeating the words "in the name of the Father, and the Son, and the Holy Spirit"? Check it out. There is not a single instance. Can you work out why they never used this formula to obey the command?

Question 3

- The apostle Paul equated the Hebrew rite of circumcision with water baptism in the New Testament (Colossians 2:10-15; Romans 2:28-29, 15:15:8-13). That is when Jewish male babies received their name even as we receive the name of the Lord Jesus Christ at our water baptism. Keeping in mind that God nearly killed Moses when he dared to proceed with God's mission in Egypt without first circumcising his sons (Exodus 4:24-26), what does that tell you about water baptism which Christians are divided about? Consider John 3:23 and what you have read about the baptism of Jesus.

- The Jews celebrate Passover by recalling the night they escaped from Egypt. Passover equates with the cross of Christ and therefore salvation. Why do you think the Lord asked the Hebrews to smear the blood on the door posts rather than on the roofs of their dwellings; that would surely have been easier to see by the death angel passing over the houses?

- What took place when they crossed the Red Sea? Did they just cross a shallow swamp? If not, why not?
- If they passed through a deep channel that collapsed onto Pharoah and his chariots, what two important things does it tell you about water baptism which Paul says is equivalent to burying the old man?
- Philip the evangelist water baptized the Ethiopian eunuch in Acts 8:38-39. Why did the Ethiopian not see Philip being transported away?
- Philip found himself at Azotus (Ashdod in Gaza). In Hebrew Azotus means "Stronghold". In the context of water baptism why do you think God translated him to Azotus rather than to any other place?

CHAPTER 9

Ignore the Old Testament at Your Peril

If western (Gentile) Christianity, Pentecostal or otherwise, thinks it has all the answers and ignores Jewry and essential elements of the Old Testament, it will never be able to fulfil the will of Jesus as expressed plainly in Ephesians chapter 4,

"Christ chose some of us to be apostles, prophets, missionaries, pastors, and teachers, so that his people would learn to serve and his body would grow strong. This will continue until we are united by our faith and by our understanding of the Son of God. Then we will be mature, just as Christ is, and we will be completely like him. We must stop acting like children. We must not let deceitful people trick us by their false teachings [spreading a cheap gospel to please the crowds], which are like winds that toss us around from place to place. Love should always make us tell the truth. Then we will grow in every way and be more like Christ, the head of the body. Christ holds it together and makes all of its parts work perfectly, as it grows and becomes strong because of love" (Ephesians 4:11–16, CEV).

Note firstly that these ascension gift ministries are to continue on planet Earth until those who are teachable grow to full maturity; not once we are in heaven but right now at this end of the age. The five-fold ministry is given not to lord over the congregation as a superior class of clergy, but to equip everyone within reach to maturity in Christ. It is only by this means that the bride of Christ will be made ready, to a state of perfection, suitable for her groom and Master. The onus is on us (Revelation 19:7). Jesus/Yeshua is waiting for us to make ourselves ready!

So many protest that that can never be, but the Word promises that it will happen towards the end. This was the purpose of God from before the beginning; it is the subject matter of the entire Bible from Genesis through to Revelation. The book of Revelation and the timing of the Second Coming can only be properly understood by referring to the Old Testament.

Any leadership team that does not have an active program to teach the young and old of the symbolism and teachings hidden in Old Testament jewels such as the Tabernacle of Moses and its rituals, multiplied in the Temple of Solomon, the significant differences between the civil and religious calendar of the Hebrews and its links to agricultural seasons, the first Passover and the pattern of 7s evident in the Feasts of Israel and the Creative and Redemptive Weeks that carry over into the book of Revelation are doing a disservice to their congregations.

Even more emphatically than that, they are robbing God and their own congregations!

At the end, the Father will recognize no one who is outside of Christ. Outsiders will be discarded by

God in the same way as is domestic refuse from a family household. They will be condemned for not having believed the Words of the Father or of the Son of God (John 3:18). In other words, they declared God a liar.

Leaderships will be embarrassed and asked why they restricted and greatly limited the Word of God in their constitutions, such as those who hold to Cessationism. Consult Dr. Google if you don't know what that means. Cessationists hold their views because of their personal experiences not because it is biblical. When we finally stand before the Father to give account of our lives, we shall be justified or condemned by the words we have spoken or written. Jesus sternly warned future generations in Matthew 12:37,

"On that day they will be told that they are either innocent or guilty because of the things they have said" (CEB). And,

"Be diligent to present yourself approved to God as a workman who does not need to be ashamed, accurately handling the word of truth" (2 Tim. 2:15, NASB).

Unfortunately, some pastors refuse to be corrected or taught, especially by lowly members of their congregations who might know some parts of the Scripture better than they do. These pastors are otherwise caring of the flock.

Such pastors are complacent in their ministry, filled with a degree of knowledge, have retirement benefits or homes waiting for them and hold the respect of many in their congregations. They often never attend Bible studies given by others in their own church. It's below them to attend. They find it incredulous that any 'insignificant' member could possibly have a word from God for them! Certainly not, not while they rule the roost — dictionary meaning *"to be the person who makes all the decisions in a group: example, in that family it is the grandma who rules the roost"* (Cambridge Dictionary definition).

Question 1

- Read Ephesians 4:11-16 carefully. Explain in your own words what the apostle is saying.
- In Romans 1:20 the apostle Paul explains that no one in the world, past or present, will ever be able to say that they didn't know that God designed the world. Will believing Christians be able to excuse themselves at the throne for not having grown further in Christ? Elaborate on your answer.

- What exhortation do we have in Scripture that we need to grow from being infants in Christ? Consider the book of Hebrews chapter 6:1-2. Can you find other encouraging examples?

Question 2

- Have you ever heard of this topic being taught from the pulpit? If not, why not? Think of a few possible reasons.
- If they were taught what observations or comments were made from the pulpit concerning this topic?
- What is your opinion now? Detail the reasons for your opinion.

Question 3

- Many people in the Bible knew what they had to do when the signs around them were clear of something to come, for example: The sons of Issachar, 1 Chronicles; Anna and Simeon knew that they would see the first coming of Jesus before they died, as did the wise men from the East. Jeremiah and Daniel knew the time of captivity in Babylon and the time of their release from Babylon. Is it therefore possible that by studying the Scripture we too ought to know the signs of the times and what to do? Comment.

CHAPTER 10

Restoration of a United Israel

B y watching testimonies on YouTube from Israel Charles was made aware only a few years ago that returning members of the ten 'lost' tribes of the once-united Israel, the northern kingdom, don't like to be called Jews. They insist that they are Israelites. The term Jew strictly refers to those in the southern kingdom belonging to Judah, Benjamin, and Levi who decided to remain in Jerusalem of Judah with king Rehoboam, son of Solomon, when the southern and northern kingdoms split. The State of Israel is mainly Jewish but a trickle of Israelites is also returning once they can establish their identities in various ways.

There are many prophecies concerning the restoration of Israel being fulfilled before our eyes, beginning with the formation of the State of Israel in 1948. Their restoration also means that the Second Coming is close at hand. We don't intend to dwell on these prophecies except to point out a few landmark scriptures relevant to Jews who believe in Christ, Yeshua our Saviour.

Converted Jews are widely referred to as "Messianic Jews" for obvious reasons. God has not forgotten those in the dispersion either. Listen how the apostle addresses the dispersed of the distant future foreknowing that they will return to God before the Second Coming: *"James, a servant of God and the Lord Jesus Christ, to the twelve tribes which are scattered abroad, Greetings"* (James 1:1, ERV). Amazing, isn't it? An epistle specifically designed to be read two thousand years later.

"I will be found by you, says the Lord, and I will return your captivity and gather you from all the nations and from all the places where I have driven you, says the Lord, and I will return you to the place where I have exiled you" (Jeremiah 29:14, ESV, and the entire chapter). Bible scholars will recognize this as a prophecy of double reference, meaning that it applies to an early fulfilment as well as to a distant future event.

There is a growing number of Israelis who once thought they were Gentiles, who are returning to Israel fulfilling end-time prophecy. They are Jews for the most part, but there are some Israelis amongst them. The insert is that of a Jewish Law of Return stamp in the passport of a returning Hebrew in 2006.

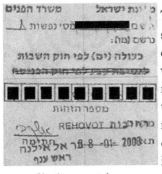

The State of Israel is suffering and there is a constant dread of being wiped out by Islamic nations. Our hope is that their sufferings may turn many to repentance. Most of its people, especially in Tel Aviv, celebrate ungodly lives with gusto while others are Zionists looking for a worldly solution, bathing in the amazing capacity of clever Israeli scientists to turn deserts green.

God's eyes are intensely focussed on Israel. The State of Israel has proven itself in several ways. God's seed was promised through Isaac not Ishmael, the son of Hagar an Egyptian woman representing worldliness and works of the flesh. Israel turned its barren lands into fruitful productivity. It is determined to reclaim lands granted to it by God Almighty in the days of Moses and Joshua, long before Mohammed and Islam came on the scene. The Koran was only published 600 years after Christ and contains corrupted extracts of the Old and New Testaments by those who rejected Christ.

Jerusalem is tightly linked to the return of Christ in Bible prophecies (Zechariah 14:1–4, 9; Matthew 24–25; Acts 1:9–12). Demon-inspired forces of Islam are attempting to delay or prevent altogether the coming of Messiah by their effort to destroy Israel. It is not just a physical battle in the Middle East as governments think. The Father foreknew that it would happen this way so do not be dismayed (Psalm 91). Satan cannot do anything Adonai won't allow. Do not miss the fact that God is using end-time events to separate the sheep from the goats (Matthew 25:32-33). Jesus promised that the evil will become worse by the hour while the good will become more righteous. So, make your choice now to progress into the Holy Place, so to speak. Be filled with the Spirit for a start and become teachable! As we have described in this book, it is God's will that Outer Court Christians be placed under great stress and faced with a momentous choice: Will they keep their faith in the Lord, or will they succumb to the temptations of the beast 666 to have an easy life if they deny Christ? The demons always fall into the Lord's snare, even as they did when they instigated the crucifixion of Christ. Satan and his mates kicked themselves afterwards (1 Corinthians 2:8). Satan's (the dragon) rage to destroy Israel and the world through wars will stop people from sitting on the fence. Everyone will have to make a decision! Make yours now.

God never abandoned Israel despite their blindness and persecutions over the past two thousand years since the destruction of Jerusalem in AD 70. This gap of two thousand years, when God turned his grace to Gentiles, is generally referred to as the "Times of the Gentiles" *or in the KJV, "Overspreading of Abominations"*; because of the continuation of blood sacrifices by the Jews since the cross (see the boxed chart below). This period is part of Daniel's 70-week prophecy (Daniel 9:24–27); the prophecy accurately predicted the timing of the First Coming. Don't be surprised, therefore, that it is possible to deduce the approximate year of the Second Coming; certainly not the hour (Matthew 24:36). The Bible has it all! The book by Charles "*End Times: According to Scripture*" explains the steps required to deduce it, but one has to be prepared to read the book because it draws on the Feasts of Israel, the symbolism in the Tabernacle of Moses, and on the longevity of the Patriarchs especially before Noah's flood, etc.

Concerning those who doubt the longevities in the book of Genesis and whether the ancients counted the length of a year differently, there can be no mistake because the Ecclesial Calendar of the Hebrews is closely tied to harvest times. For example, Passover is held at the ripening of the first fruits of barley, Pentecost to wheat and Tabernacles in the 7th month is tied to the harvest of summer fruits such as olives, dates, grapes etc. Tabernacles has much to tell us about end-times. However, one needs to read informative books to appreciate these gems.

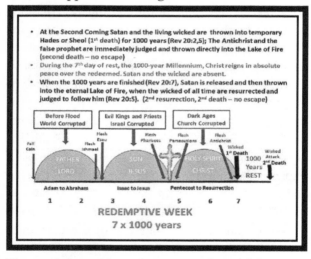

- At the Second Coming Satan and the living wicked are thrown into temporary Hades or Sheol (1st death) for 1000 years (Rev 20:2,5); The Antichrist and the false prophet are immediately judged and thrown directly into the Lake of Fire (second death – no escape)
- During the 7th day of rest, the 1000-year Millennium, Christ reigns in absolute peace over the redeemed. Satan and the wicked are absent.
- When the 1000 years are finished (Rev 20:7), Satan is released and then thrown into the eternal Lake of Fire, when the wicked of all time are resurrected and judged to follow him (Rev 20:5). (2nd resurrection, 2nd death – no escape)

Before Flood World Corrupted	Evil Kings and Priests Israel Corrupted	Dark Ages Church Corrupted

Fall Cain — Flesh Ishmael — Flesh Esau — Flesh Pharisees — Flesh Persecutions — Flesh Antichrist — Wicked 1st Death — Wicked Attack 2nd Death

FATHER LORD / SON JESUS / HOLY SPIRIT CHRIST / 1000 Years REST

Adam to Abraham | Isaac to Jesus | Pentecost to Resurrection

1   2   3   4   5   6   7

REDEMPTIVE WEEK
7 x 1000 years

The truth be told, we have never heard Messianic Jews confessing to the public at length that the Jews brought their diaspora upon themselves, "*When Pilate saw that he was accomplishing nothing, but rather that a riot was starting, he took water and washed his hands in front of the crowd, saying, "I am innocent of this Man's blood; see to that yourselves."* And all the people said, *"His blood shall be on us and on our children!"'* (Matthew 27:24–25, NASB). Even Gentile churches avoid the subject for fear of offending the Jews.

On Palm Sunday Christians celebrate the entry of Jesus on the foal of a donkey with everyone crying "Hosannah" as they waved palm leaves. That custom was reserved for heroes of Israel, such as the Maccabees 150 years earlier when they liberated Jerusalem from the Greeks. In the case of Jesus, the crowds cried out before Pilate *"Crucify Him"* only three days after they welcomed him. Why? They were disappointed that Yeshuah cleansed the Temple instead of demanding Pilate to liberate Israel from Roman rule. The populace wasn't interested in being liberated from their sins.

Orthodox Jews have the same expectation today, awaiting the coming of a deliverer to liberate them from Hamas, ISIS, Hezboliah, the Iranians etc. They think that building a structure out of stone and resuming sacrifices will please God. What is Prime Minister Netenyahu doing? Exactly that: Trying to clean up Gaza militarily despite being short of sufficient resources, having to depend on other countries for its air defence such as the USA, Britain, Jordan and the UAR, the latter two being Islamic countries. How long will they remain neutral yet support Israel over their own airspace? Israel is daily embattled in conflict with Iran for a good reason. It is being fought physically but there are demonic forces that rule over Iran and their accomplices behind it all; the Spirit of Christ versus the Spirit of Babylon. Amazingly, governments are oblivious as to what is really happening behind the scenes.

An old Jewish pattern is repeating itself by those in power: A zeal for liberation from aggression, but generally no interest in liberation from sin.

Jews Must Repent Even as Must Gentiles

"When that day comes, Adonai will defend those living in Yerushalayim. On that day, even someone who stumbles will be like David; and the house of David will be like God, like the angel of Adonai before them. "When that day comes, I will seek to destroy all nations attacking Yerushalayim; and I will pour out on the house of David

and on those living in Yerushalayim a spirit of grace and prayer; and they will look to me, whom they pierced." They will mourn for him as one mourns for an only son; they will be in bitterness on his behalf like the bitterness for a firstborn son. When that day comes, there will be great mourning in Yerushalayim, mourning like that for Hadad-Rimmon in the Megiddo Valley. Then the land will mourn, each family by itself—the family of the house of David by itself, and their wives by themselves; the family of the house of Natan by itself, and their wives by themselves; the family of the house of Levi by itself, and their wives by themselves; the family of the Shim'I by itself, and their wives by themselves; all the remaining families, each by itself, and their wives by themselves" (Zechariah 12:8–14, JCB).

Only then will repentant Jews shine with the glory of the Lord as a sizable number already do, *"Arise, shine [Yerushalayim], for your light has come, the glory of Adonai has risen over you. For although darkness covers the earth and thick darkness the peoples; on you Adonai will rise; over you will be seen his glory. Nations will go toward your light and kings toward your shining splendor. Raise your eyes and look around: they are all assembling and coming to you; your sons are coming from far off, your daughters being carried on their nurses' hips.*

Then you will see and be radiant, your heart will throb and swell with delight; for the riches of the seas will be brought to you, the wealth of nations will come to you" (Isaiah 60:1–5, CJB).

CHAPTER 11

Message and Power of the 'Chuppah'

CHARLES & GLORIA JORIM PALLAGHY

A Chuppah, "canopy" or "covering" in Hebrew, is a canopy under which a Jewish couple stand during their wedding ceremony. It consists of a delicate cloth or sheet, usually a white lace, stretched or supported over four poles, or sometimes manually held up by attendants at the ceremony. The Chuppah symbolizes the home that the couple will build together.

Just as a Chuppah is open on all four sides, so was the tent of Abraham open for hospitality. Thus, the Chuppah represents hospitality to one's guests. This "home" initially lacks furniture as a reminder that the basis of a Jewish home is the people within it, not the possessions. In a spiritual sense, the covering of the Chuppah represents the presence of God over the covenant of marriage. The Chuppah was erected to signify that the ceremony and institution of marriage has divine origins (extracted from Wikipedia, https://en.wikipedia.org/wiki/Chuppah).

That is essentially all that the reader might find on the net about the Chuppah itself. A Chuppah is typically tastefully decorated with flowers. We were married under a Chuppah because we wanted our marriage to be symbolically blessed. We also wanted a marriage with a Jewish flavour. Charles purchased a cubic gazebo from a hardware store and painted it white.

Charles explained during his response at the wedding feast that Orthodox Jews don't understand, from a spiritual point of view, why they do what they do – why they religiously repeat their rituals year after year. In contrast, Messianic Jews are so  enthusiastic that they have created some wonderful YouTube programs that the world needs to hear. The peculiarities of the Passover Meal, the Seder, point to the crucifixion of Jesus. At the Seder, they recant events of the first Passover in Egypt and do things that probably mystify them.

What is the message of the Chuppah that God wants us to know about? Its message will only make sense to those willing to look at both the Old and New Testaments in some detail. After all, the entire

Bible is to do with Christ (the anointed one) so it's no surprise that it should highlight Christ wherever one looks. That surely implies that the answers to our questions can be found there. We have done that and have chosen to look carefully and analyze relevant verses in context.

It is evident that unconverted Jews don't realize what their rituals might mean concerning heavenly realities. Hebrews chapter 10 verse 7 records what Jesus said about himself: "*Then said I, Lo, I come (in the volume of the book it is written of me,) to do thy will, O God*" (Hebrews 10:7). We should, therefore, pay serious attention to what might appear to be boring details in sections of the Bible. They are there for particular purposes!

Let's begin with the characteristically cubic structure of a Chuppah. Why are they cubic? To answer that, we need to merge our Jewish faith and knowledge of the Tanakh with what Gentile Christians have been teaching ever since Christ was crucified outside the walls of Jerusalem. In the God-anointed temples that were built since the days of the Exodus, God always made his presence known in a heavily covered compartment that was cubic in shape, in the Tabernacle of Moses and in Solomon's Temple. The cube was known as the Most Holy Place, or the Holiest of Holies as explained in Chapter 8. The only light in the Most Holy Place was the Shekinah glory of God shining forth from between the two golden cherubim on the Mercy Seat of the Ark of the Covenant. This was also the case in the large permanent temple constructed much later by King David's son Solomon; the dimensions of the Most Holy Place were double those in the Tabernacle of Moses. Solomon's Temple, the Second Temple, had 10 candlesticks and 10 lavers in the Outer Court instead instead of only one. Herod's Temple, familiar to Jesus was bigger in layout than either of them but its Most Holy Place, missing the Ark lost centuries earlier, was also cubic.

The New Jerusalem talked about in the 66 books of the Bible is not a rebuilt City of Jerusalem on Earth. Our New Jerusalem, the city of God, is in the Paradise to come (Revelation 3:12; 21:2, 16). God promised to dwell there with His people forever. The symbolic dimensions of the New Jerusalem are also those of a perfect cube (Revelation 21:16). One can recognise that the dimensions are symbolic, because each side measures about 2000 km and its foundations are twelve apostles.

God uses the symbolism of a perfect geometric structure to imply that He is perfect and holy. Therefore, stretching right through from the period of the Law to the end of the "Times of the Gentiles," and into the Millennium covering a period of 4500 years (1500 + 2000 + 1000 years), God has chosen to communicate with mankind within a symbolic cubic structure even in the New Jerusalem in eternity, at least symbolically. "*The same yesterday, today and tomorrow*" (Hebrews 13:8). The cube with its three perfect dimensions also testifies that our one God is a triune God—Father, Son and Holy Spirit, three persons as one. Before his incarnation in human flesh in the womb of Mary, the son was the eternal Word (John Chapter 1). The Holy Spirit is a person. Note the personal pronouns Jesus employs about the Holy Spirit in John 14:26, 16:13-15.

We believe this to be the forgotten reason why the Chuppah is associated with the divine. Not only that, but the city of the New Jerusalem is declared in symbolic form to be synonymous with the perfected bride of Christ in Revelation 21:9, "'*Then one of the seven angels who had the seven bowls full of the seven last plagues came to me and said, "Come! I will show you the bride, the wife of the lamb*" (Revelation 21:9, KJV). This city is shining with "Sun-glory" even as the apostle promised she would shine in her perfected state, "*That he might present it to himself a glorious church, not having spot, or wrinkle, or any such thing; but that it should be holy and without blemish*" (Ephesians 5:27, KJV).

The bride is comprised of people intimately devoted to God which cannot be said of all Christians. Hal Oxley, founder of Christian Life Church in Melbourne, in his 2001 book "*Being*" illustrated the life of many Christians using the parable of pilgrims on a long journey. Many pilgrims in Christ never reach their God-planned destinations but camp out early in their journey to enjoy the comforts and the security of their current spiritual state – no hassles no persecution. Why? Because following Christ is always associated with some degree of suffering, even as our Lord Jesus suffered throughout his three-and-a-half-year ministry, life-long criticism and animosity from one's own relatives being one example.

Such generally are unteachable disciples, if they can be generously called "disciples" who avoid all manner of discipline or correction or challenges to leave their worldly lifestyles and ungodly habits. The book of

Revelation refers to such as 'Outer Court' believers unwilling to move on.

Significantly, the Chuppah is always supported by four poles to uphold its flimsy structure. These poles symbolize the four books in the Bible which focus on critical aspects about the bride of Christ—who she is, the exhortation to go on unto perfection, how this will be achieved, and the Sun-glory of the bride of Christ once she has made herself ready.

The Song of Songs or Songs of Solomon is an allegory of the bride of Christ and her lover the Lord Jesus. Amongst all the fair virgins in the land she is the only one he seeks,

"There are threescore queens, and fourscore concubines, and virgins without number. My dove, my undefiled is but one; she is the only one of her mother, she is the choice one of her that bare her. The daughters saw her, and blessed her; yea, the queens and the concubines, and they praised her" (Songs 6:8-9). The mother referred to in this case is Jerusalem, *"the mother of us all"* (Galatians 4:26).

In addition to the Song of Songs, Ephesians, Hebrews and Revelation contain much of value for those who desire to participate in the bride.

Her lover has his eyes only on her despite all the lovely and noble virgins (the redeemed) that Jerusalem (the church) can potentially offer. The Lord lifts the Shulamite woman high up above all others, if you can catch the symbolism here.

"These are the ones who were not defiled with women, for they are virgins. These are the ones who follow the Lamb wherever He goes. These were redeemed from among men, being firstfruits to God and to the Lamb" (Revelation 14:4). What women? In Bible code "women" often symbolise churches, and in our context women (churches) who spread a watered-down gospel.

At the wedding, Charles explained another significant signature under the Chuppah. At one stage during the ceremony, the bride encircles the groom seven times. Why is that? It's to be a reminder for those, who live in the end times as we do today, that through the bride of Christ Jesus will have absolute victory over his enemies. Seven times takes us back to the church in the wilderness who after forty years of wandering are finally allowed to enter the Promised Land, the land of milk and honey.

Are they allowed to just walk in and displace the Canaanites who worshipped other gods and sacrificed children? No, they had to fight to take the land, not with physical weapons but by simply believing God for victory. At the command of Joshua, the people were to have priests blowing shofars at the head of the column and all of them were to encircle the city of Jericho in absolute silence once a day for 6 days, but on the 7th day they were to encircle the city walls 7 times. Then they gave a massive shout and the walls collapsed. Note the prominence of the number 7, an indicator that this event is relevant to the people of God who live in the end times. Christ and His bride shall triumph likewise over the Earth in the final harvest (Rev. 22.17). Our wedding was marked with a brief blow on the shofar.

Question

- How does this chapter verify the need for merging Messianic Jews and Gentile Christians? Jot down a few points that come to mind. Then enlarge on each point.

- Is there anything new that you have learnt that stands out?

CHAPTER 12

What Can We Say Therefore?

The final message of this book is that Christ shall complete His mandate under the Father to build His Church. Messianic Jews and Gentile Christians must appreciate to act in unison, to realize that they both belong to one and the same Spiritual Israel. As Paul said, there is neither a Jew or a Gentile if we are in Christ.

> *"There is neither Jew nor Greek… for ye are all one in Christ"* **(Galatians 3:28). And again in Colossians 3:11 the apostle said,** *"there is neither Greek nor Jew, circumcision nor uncircumcision… but Christ is all, and in all"*.

Note the reversal of Jew and Greek in the two versions to emphasize that neither is to be the head. Messianic Jews sometimes ought to humbly acknowledge in their programs, especially on TV, that they owe their faith to Gentile Christianity from whom they first received the gospel of Jesus Christ. Their Jewish Messiah, Yeshua, was hidden from them until the Times of the Gentiles, the 2000-year growth of Gentile Christianity that is coming to an end as foretold in Daniel's 70-week prophesy (Daniel Chapter 9).

Charles had a German mother, but the Pallaghy family had many good Jewish, Hungarian and German friends but avoided the arrogant. The point we are making is that Jews are no better or worse than the Gentile nations. God is, and shall be, a blessing to Jerusalem not because the Jews are more wonderful than other peoples but because the Lord put His name there forever (Psalm 132:13-14; 137:5-6; 2 Kings 21:7; 2 Chronicles 12:13)!

It is consistent with the biblical fact that God shall not intervene against the foreign armies of Armaggedon in their systematic destruction of Israel, until they come to the walls of Jerusalem, the city of God, the city of peace (Luke 21:20-23). Only then will God take His vengeance by destroying the heathen armies utterly.

The topography of Jerusalem reveals the name of the Messiah as though God had carved it into the landscape; doubtless, He did! Three significant valleys viewed from above form the 21st letter of the Hebrew alphabet in print block form, 'shin'. Its numerical value is 300. Shin means peace, to be seen, and is identified with the name of the Lord. We encourage readers interested in the gematria of the Hebrew language to view, "*Secret of the Hebrew letter shin reveals the Messiah. Evidence of design in the original Hebrew text of the Bible*". https://youtu.be/gX24yJR6DY8

שמה הוש

Shin is not just any Hebrew letter. "*In Hebrew, this letter stands for one of the names of God. El Shadaii, the Almighty. It also stands for Shalom, the common Jewish greeting which means "perfect peace."*

It is also the first letter in the Shekinah the *Ruach Ha Kodesh*, the consuming fire, and amazingly enough the letter also looks like a fire.

שמה הוש

The Shin is also the letter printed on the Mezuzah, that graces the doorpost of every Jewish home. The photo is a close- up of a typical Mezuzah in Jerusalem. The Jews literally obey the command of God to bind the law of God onto their doorposts. In every Jewish home there is a Mezuzah beside the doorway. When they leave their home, they touch this Mezuzah and kiss their fingertips. Why? On the Mezuzah is the letter Shin to represent the name of God and inside the Mezuzhah is a tiny scroll on which is written, "*Hear O Israel, the Lord our God is*

One Lord......." (Deuteronomy 6:4-9). When they leave home, they touch that letter that represents the name of God, and kiss their fingertips as a sign of reverence to God and His word.

The letter Shin is also represented by a finger V sign occasionally during Jewish synagogue services. Most will recognize this hand sign made famous by Spock from Star Treck. Being a Jew Leonard Nemoy, who played Spock, came up with this hand sign himself. When Moses was up on the mountain during the battle with the Amalekites (Exodus 17:11-12) whenever he lifted his hands the Hebrews won, but when he lowered his hands they were beaten. The Berean Bible Journeys on the internet explains that by lifting his hands his upper torso assumed the shape of the Shin. https://bereanbiblejourneys.com/the-letter-shin/

Pride and pre-eminence have no place in the bride of Christ who will be comprised of Messianic Jewry, Messianic Israelites and Christian Gentiles. In any case, Israeli DNA from the ten northern 'lost tribes', is not Jewish as explained in our book, is dispersed throughout the Gentile nations because of millennia of interbreeding.

MERGING JEW AND GENTILE FOR PERFECTION

This is what the apostle Paul, a Hebrew of Hebrews from the tribe of Benjamin, had to say about his own people in Romans 10:15-21, *"But they have not all obeyed the gospel. For Isaiah says, 'Lord, who has believed our report?' So then, faith comes by hearing, and hearing by the word of God. But I say, have they not heard? Yes indeed: 'Their sound has gone out throughout the earth, and their words to the end of the world.'*

"But I say, did Israel not know? First Moses says: 'I will provoke you to jealousy by those who are no people, and by a foolish nation I will anger you.' But Isaiah is very bold and says: 'I was found by those who did not seek me; I became known to those who did not ask after Me.' But to Israel he says: 'All day long I have stretched forth my hands to a disobeying and contrary people'" (MKJV).

Israel a World-wide Stink: Armageddon

There are interesting parallels between recent events in the modern State of Israel and the biblical accounts of the rape of Jacob's only daughter, Dinah, and Samson's final victory over the Philistines, arch enemies of Israel.

Before meeting with his brother Esau, whom Jacob had
cheated by lying to Isaac their father, Jacob wrestled
all night with the angel of God and was given his new
name, Israel. "*And Jacob was left alone. A Man wrestled
there with him until the breaking of the day. And when
He saw that He did not prevail against him, He touched
the hollow of his thigh. And the hollow of Jacob's thigh
was out of joint as he wrestled with Him. And He said,
let Me go, for the day breaks. (Jacob) said, I will not let
you go except you bless me. He said to him, what is your
name? And he said to Jacob, your name shall no longer be
called Jacob, but Israel; for like a prince you have power
with God and with men and have prevailed. Jacob asked
and said, I pray You, reveal Your name. And He said, why
do you ask after My name? He blessed him there. And
Jacob called the name of the place Face of God; for I have
seen God face to face, and my life is preserved*" (Genesis
32:24-30, MKJV).

Bible scholars have included such events under
the general heading of "Jacob's Trouble" in line
with Jeremiah's prophecy in Chapter 30 verses 4-7.
The verses describe Jacob bowing and humbling
himself 7-times to Esau (Israel bowing to the world,
prophetically speaking). As it is in every single case,
the number 7 also ties the event to end times. Jacob's

young daughter was raped by a Canaanite while she was in the fields enjoying herself. The Canaanites afterwards negotiated with Jacob for Dinah to be married to the rapist to which Jacob's twelve sons agreed. They tricked the Canaanites to circumcise themselves and then, while they were in great pain they murdered them and their families. Trembling with fear Jacob said to Simeon and Levi, *"You have troubled me, to make me stink among those who live in the land, among the Canaanites and the Perizzites. And I, being few in number, they shall gather themselves together against me, and kill me. And I shall be destroyed, my house and I"* (Genesis 34:30, MKJV).

In the Hebrew tongue 'Dinah' means 'justice, God's revenge', which would have also been an appropriate name for Samson's legal wife whom the Philistines murdered along with her father and household (Judges 15:6).

Rape, kidnap and forced marriage of young girls has been typical of the violent methods of ISIS in Africa against Christian girls. Hamas carried out similar violations in their unprecedented attack against Israel on October 7th, 2023, killing 1,139 people: 695 Israeli civilians (including 36 children), publicly torturing and humiliating them by stripping them naked on the streets of Gaza in front of cheering and delighted Palestinian crowds. The most recent mass attack by Iran using approximately 300 drones and missiles illustrates the intention of radical Islam to wipe Israel off the map. The world quickly forgot how much the Palestinian public rejoiced and sided with the sufferings of the Palestinians instead of with Israel. The world hates Judeo-Christianity (Matthew 10:22; Mark 13:13; Luke 21:17; John 17:14) because they hate the works of God.

God seems to use such events to goad his enemies to gather in mass against Jerusalem and Israel before destroying the heathen armies. Iran must be frustrated that the air forces of USA, UK, Jordan and the UAR combined to down most of the drones and missiles before they reached Israeli airspace.

Another example of God goading the enemy to their destruction is when the Philistines gathered in Gaza to watch the public humiliation of Samson (Judges 14:4;),

"Then the lords of the Philistines gathered in order to offer a great sacrifice to Dagon their god, and to rejoice. For they said, our god has delivered Samson our enemy into our hand. The people saw him and praised their god. For they said, our god has delivered

our enemy into our hand, and the destroyer of our country, who killed many of us. When their hearts were merry, it happened that they said, call for Samson and he will make sport for us.

And they called for Samson out of the prison house. And he made sport for them, and they set him between the pillars. Samson said to the lad who held him by the hand, Allow me to feel the pillars upon which the house stands, so that I may lean upon them. Now the house was full of men and women. All the lords of the Philistines were there. On the roof were about three thousand men and women who watched while Samson made sport.

Samson called to Jehovah and said, O, Lord Jehovah, remember me, I pray You, and strengthen me, I pray You, only this once, O God, so that I may be at once avenged of the Philistines for my two eyes. Samson took hold of the two middle pillars upon which the house stood, and on which it was held up, of the one with his right hand, and of the other with his left. And Samson said, let me die with the Philistines. And he bowed himself mightily, and the house fell upon the lords and upon all the people in it. The dead whom he killed at his death were more than those he killed in his life" (Judges 16:23-30, MKJV).

Furthermore, we have the example when Pharaoh's army was goaded into following the Hebrews into the opened channel in the Gulf of Aqaba after God removed the cloud of fire (representing the Holy Spirit). All his army was drowned shattering the might of Egypt forever, and in the outpouring of the 7 bowls upon an evil world at the end (Revelation 16:1-16). We annotated the map.

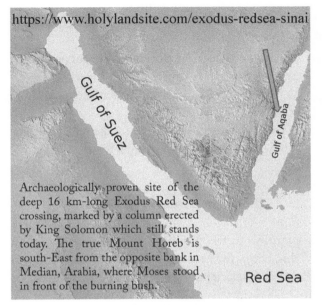

https://www.holylandsite.com/exodus-redsea-sinai

Gulf of Suez

Gulf of Aqaba

Archaeologically proven site of the deep 16 km-long Exodus Red Sea crossing, marked by a column erected by King Solomon which still stands today. The true Mount Horeb is south-East from the opposite bank in Median, Arabia, where Moses stood in front of the burning bush.

Red Sea

Question 1

- What local factors influence the measure of your faith where you live?
- Do you turn to friends rather than to the shepherds (pastors) to resolve your problems?
- If you answered in the affirmative give your reasons for not wanting to talk to the ministry responsible for your care (John 10:11; John 21:17).

Question 2

- Do great melodies and a good choir influence where you attend?
- Do you enjoy some form of entertainment performed on the church platform?
- Where in your list of priorities are systematic Bible studies?
- If you have answered Questions 1 and 2 honestly, what does it reveal about yourself?

Repentance from False Doctrines

According to the prophetic warnings of Jonathan Cahn, Harry the man of God from Thessalonica and Rabbi Schneider in 2024, America may be no more in 2025. Johnathan Cahn and Rabbi Schneider are Messianic Jews worth listening to. Harry the prophet has proven himself too. In a dream Harry saw masses of enemy submarines entering American waters. Whether one chooses to believe the dream or not is beside the point. We all know that the USA is in deep trouble. All three have urgently called/implied to the American public and the churches to repent. Repent in what sense, you might ask? Is it to do with American politics? Perhaps, but it runs much deeper than that.

America started off well and in God they put their trust until most States removed God from every phase of public life. America has become lawless, is torn between two presidential candidates and is depending on elections to return to the glorious nation they once were. Unimpeded rage and gun violence rules the land. The White House is powerless because of the many layers of government. Looming clouds of civil war darken the land. Their government is godless.

God is threatening to wipe America out in the same way that He threatened to wipe out Nineveh that great ancient Assyrian city in the days of Jonah. Nineveh repented from the king down to the basest of servants and God's threats were averted!

We cannot imagine God expecting all of America to repent in the same way: In the days of Nineveh all people believed that a god or gods existed, and Jonah's appearance frightened them into action. That is no longer the case in Western Nations. Creationism had to be the focus of evangelism last century to first introduce the existence of God to a faithless Western world.

In one of my websites, www.creation6000.com (our website highlighting reviews on our books is www.endtimespallaghy.com), I illustrated that there is only one true aspect to evolution theory: the theory of '*Microevolution*'. Ironically, *Microevolution* is not only factual and the outcome of genetic laws, but textbooks deliberately reduce this factual aspect of evolution to a "theory" in the hope that students will elevate in their minds the fanciful theory of *Macroevolution* to the same level. It is Satan's ploy to confuse university students, teachers, the media and laypeople alike.

Microevolution accounts for the limited diversification of species possible through environmental and other factors. Plant and animal breeders have been using these methods for millennia. The original kind of animal (or plant) that walked off Noah's Ark can be changed into new forms either by environmental conditions or breeders, such as the huge varieties of dogs or the wild Australian dingo in existence today. Regardless of the form (phenotype) of the new dog breeds, some of which are incapable of interbreeding because of size differences, even science recognizes them as belonging to the same species *Canis familiaris*. Charles Darwin in his book on the *Origin of Species* knew all about *Microevolution* because he was familiar with the vast numbers of pigeon varieties that were bred in his day. Because of his limited knowledge and distrust of the clergy and the Bible, he proposed the fanciful idea of '*Macroevolution*', a term not coined by him. Macroevolution is the theory of quantum leaps in their DNA content such as wingless creatures developing wings and feathers over eons of time; or whales evolving from four footed land creatures and so on. Not even the Australian duck-billed platypus that spends most of its time underwater in rivers is a mammal. It is a furry egg laying creature that produces milk, has poisonous barbs, a flat tail like a beaver and the feet of an otter. The platypus will remain a mystery to science until the Second Coming. It shares DNA with reptiles, birds and mammals mystifying evolutionary scientists. In face of all the evidence contrary to evolution theory, such as Michael Denton's 1985 book *Evolution: A Theory in Crisis*, educational institutions refuse to acknowledge a Creator God. I and a friend visited Michael Denton one day because his laboratory was in a building adjacent to mine. I asked him, "*Now that you have proven all the current theories of evolution wrong, what other option is there for life to have originated on Earth?*" He responded frankly, "*I don't know. I can't think of anything else*". This he said, even though he could read and thoroughly understand the ancient languages of the Hebrews and the Greeks. He even said that the Jews missed the Messiah when it was obviously Jesus according to the Old Testament prophecies. He is a clear case of someone who has all the evidence before him, but his eyes cannot see past the natural. Most university educators are equally spiritually blind.

We doubt whether the entire United States is capable of repenting. We remember the three angels, Epiphanes of the Trinity, coming to Abraham before they went down to destroy Sodom and Gomorrah (Genesis Chapter 18). Abraham attempted to negotiate leniency and mercy because of his nephew Lot who lived there with his wife and daughters. In the end the Lord agreed that he would not destroy the cities if he found at least ten righteous inhabitants, which he didn't. The same would seem to apply to the USA. **The Lord is surely only seeking faithful people throughout the USA to pray and repent if they have been following doctrinally liberal churches or false leaders for one reason or another.**

Believing in the existence of the one and only Mighty God is not the only battleground that people struggle with. The large number of false teachers on YouTube, not rightly dividing the word of God, are an even greater danger to Christianity. The greatest danger comes from within the church; Judas was a prime example. Compelling false teachers with large followings have infiltrated the mindset of masses of Christians, Jews (Messianic) and Gentiles alike. Too many Christians have never studied the differences between symbolism, poetry and allegories to be able to distinguish certain scriptures from those that were meant to be literally understood. Self-appointed false teachers have surfaced everywhere including in official Bible Schools (2 Peter 2:1). I have met several of them personally and am astounded by what they are permitted to teach.

Some false 'Messianic' teachers on YouTube, wearing Jewish garb to impress, entice both Christian (Messianic) Jews and Gentiles to go back and serve the shadows of the Law, instead of causing us to rejoice in the liberties of the New Covenant which the Lamb of God secured for us through the resurrection (Acts 15:24-33).

There is a pattern to their teachings that one can lookout for. Although truth and grace came by Jesus Christ (Yeshuah), the Law was only annulled once

Yeshua was resurrected. Jesus had to fulfil every jot and title of the Law, including the five Levitical offerings (the Whole Burnt Offering, the Grain Offering, the Peace Offering, the Sin Offering and the Trespass Offering), to be an acceptable sacrifice for the atonement of our sins. During His life, and in the Garden of Gethsemane and on the cross, Yeshua had to fulfil every jot and title of the Law which is why He became the one and only acceptable blood offering to the Father. This is important! Until the resurrection Jesus and his disciples lived during the dispensational period known as the Law which began in the days of Moses about 1500 years before Christ.

False Messianic teachers tend to quote from the gospels which in essence were lived out by Christ and his disciples under the Laws of Moses. Some of the statements of Jesus were meant for the period they lived in, not for the New Covenant. Therefore, we need to take care how we read the gospels.

Judaizers, whom the apostles had to strive against, virtually ignore or give little attention to what Paul and the apostles established in the book of Acts and in the epistles after the resurrection. The apostles appointed multiple elderships in fellowships that held communion, with no affiliation to Synagogues, such as the seven churches in the book of Revelation. Nor do they discuss scriptures which abolished the necessity of eating only Kosher foods. Our warning is not only to beware of false doctrines but to withdraw from practising them. Satan's strategy has always been to quote half-truths as he also did in the Garden of Eden and when he tempted Christ in the wilderness. Half-truths clothe glib false teachers with apparent authority that many Christians seem to willingly fall for (Galatians 3:1-3). Paul had no hesitation to call their followers in Galatia "*foolish*". Let us not be found amongst those when Christ returns.

Church Leaderships Need to Repent

Gloria and I have had terrible experiences in some churches both in Papua New Guinea, in Australia and in the USA. Gloria already mentioned in this book the cruelty she and her children endured from some male pastors in PNG over a period of five years. She has forgiven them, but the memories remain. Gloria and I have also met a mixed bag of pastors from PNG ministering in Australia covering a wide spectrum from the conniving and despicable to those that have a heart for the sheep under their charge. I couldn't believe what they can get up to away from the scrutiny of their denominations back home.

The misdemeanours of the worst seem to be tied to the love of money and exercising control over the flock. One such pastor frequently threatened Australians he contacted that God would shorten their lives if they didn't support his travel needs. Another one, who hacked my confidential emails to my children in Australia and distributed them to all the PNG contacts on Gloria's phone, exercised control over his congregation by listening in to their conversations and texts. I contacted a criminal lawyer concerning this pastor but was advised that it would be a difficult case, so Gloria advised me to forgive and forget and to pray for him instead. His own church has now sent him to a remote settlement to begin a church there.

Unfortunately, some Australian churches are no better. Many have been burnt by churches who started exceedingly well, but in the end turned out to be equally greedy and power hungry. Adhering to a prosperity gospel platform, which to me is no different to the indulgences that priests were selling in the days of Martin Luther, has caused many to leave their churches some of whom have become scattered and forlorn sheep in our community.

I, Charles, attended one church for 40 years who presented a pure gospel and wonderful O.T. teachings back in 1976 but now don't even practise communion anymore. They exercised control by saying that we couldn't do what we wanted to do but had to obey them otherwise we would go to hell. Their manner of control was to dominate our lives by insisting that they had the mind of the Lord for us not we ourselves. Whenever I wanted to query their scriptures which drove their agenda their typical response was for us to fellowship about it in private in the presence of two or three of the elders. I knew what that meant. They would grill me in private and tell me how wrong I was.

They wrecked my son's life, and I didn't know about it for years except that I couldn't understand why he was in such a bad mood all the time. I made the huge error of telling him to listen to the elders. They put the 'fear of God' in him not to tell his parents because it was a private matter between him, them and the Lord. They controlled his life. It made me think of the Nicolatian doctrine that the Lord hated as did the church at Ephesus (Revelation 2:6). Once I realized

215

that we were in a cult I shared in an open prophecy and then in letters a dream that the Lord had given me about them.

In this vision I saw the entrance to a coal mine that had tracks for coal wagons. My eyes were drawn to a wagon that had men bound in chains around their hands and necks sitting  three-a -breast in the wagon. They had long hair and had inverted crowns pressed over their heads with the prongs of their crowns biting into their necks. I was given to understand that these were men who once had authority over their flock but had abused their mandate. They were completely silent aware of their misspent ministries. As I watched, the wagons slowly descended into the dark. When I repeated the prophecy in two letters over a period of two months, together with a sketch of the vision, the arrogant eldership simply ignored me.

I am certain that there would be examples of abusive churches in any nation. I was astounded how a congregation in Florida despicably mistreated the wonderful Messianic singer Elihana Elia and her mother Dr. Hadassah when they turned up at their service. They were physically manhandled, evicted and booed by the elders and the congregation. If any of our readers were present, we hope that you had the sense to flee from that church.

After having visited and worked in the USA several times I felt that this adage is true about the nation, *"America has the worst and the best of everything"*. I am confident that this applies to their churches as well. I certainly experienced some of them during my stay, some of the best and the worst. How pleasant was the glory of the Lord in the best.

Our admonition is that anyone becoming aware of their church progressively becoming worldly and falling into apostasy, as the apostles warned would happen, then please repent from ever having participated in it and flee to a solid word-oriented church. Sometimes the evidence is abundantly clear; such as a mega church providing Bollywood-style entertainment with skimpy outfits for its Christmas show disregarding what Christmas was about. We are ignorant of the state of the Messianic churches in Israel but their worship songs and productions on YouTube have given us much joy.

Questions

There are many who avoid attending church ever again because of hurts they experienced in the past. If you are one of them, think about the following and jot down your responses:

- Would Jesus, Yeshua, want you to respond like that?
- Did the apostles set up deacons and ministers of the gospels in the New Testament church of their own accord or because of the will of the Father?
- How are you going to meet any of the five ascension gift ministries Christ gave to the church until he returns (Apostle, prophet, pastor teacher and evangelist) if you don't attend a solid teaching church somewhere?
- Does a total lack of taking communion amongst the collective place you in danger of what Jesus said, "*Unless you eat of my flesh and drink of my blood, there is no life in you*"? Communion works both

ways - communion with God and communion with fellow believers.

- Who are you going to look towards for unforeseen future events such as weddings, funerals and baptism of your children?
- Read these questions and your responses perhaps once a week and see whether God has spoken to you about it in the meanwhile.

The Thrust of Our Books

Our/my books have been written to address a repentant world to the glory that lies ahead of truly committed Christians who become overcomers and endure to the end. The Lord shall have a bride without wrinkle, spot or blemish and shining with Sun-glory regardless of what end times might bring. Four books of the Bible, including Revelation, promise a great harvest and an ingathering of a people who have prepared themselves for the coming of the Lord, as did the five wise virgins in the parable told by Jesus. These five virgins had made themselves ready for the impending marriage of the lamb. The onus is on us to remain faithful in these hours of darkness. Our website www. endtimespallaghy.com lists our current books if you are interested in further details, especially my book on End Times.

"Then I heard something like the voice of a great multitude, and like the roar of many waters and something like the sound of powerful thunder, saying, 'Hallelujah! For the Lord our God, the Almighty reigns. Let us rejoice and be glad and give him the glory, for the marriage of the Lamb has come, and his wife has made herself ready; And it has been granted to her to be clothed with bright, clean, fine linen for the fine linen is the righteous deeds of the holy ones" (Revelation 19:6-8).

"The Spirit and the bride say, 'Come'; And let the one who hears say, 'Come'; And let the one who is thirsty come; let the one who wishes, take the water of life freely" (Revelation 22:17).

CHAPTER 13

Let the Love of God Rule Our Hearts: Lessons from Our Marriage

I tried desperately not to write a thirteenth Chapter because 13 is Bible code for sin. Some hotels avoid having a 13th floor naming it 12A but the reality is that if one is allocated to 12A one is on the 13th floor. Christians like to use the numbers eight and seven thinking that they will be blessed because of it. Good numbers make us feel good.

In our case, having a 13th Chapter is poignant because we are going to deal with a sin that we must all overcome if we aspire to be as perfect as our Saviour before the resurrection. My Czech born mother-in-law, whom we used to lovingly call Babi, was a classic example of exercising partial love throughout her life. I used to hate that because her daughter to whom I was married was exactly the same.

Babi would do anything for her own relatives and grandchildren but when faced with a request to help a stranger or anyone outside the family she would ask, *"Why should I?"* The Bible speaks strongly against partiality, but we don't wish to fill up our book with more biblical quotes. Classic examples in Scripture are the parable of the good Samaritan, that God sends his rain upon both the righteous and the wicked, and when we fall into the shameful habit of reserving the best seat in church or the best possible food at our homes for a person accustomed to finery.

Religiosity, especially as expressed by those zealous for God, has caused much harm. Charles remembers a sad day when he met a grief-stricken stranger hoping to witness to him. The man immediately questioned God's love. He said that both his sons died in a car accident. Nobody in the family were church goers. He visited a local church to ask them whether they would conduct a funeral service for his sons. The answer was an immediate no because they were not members of the congregation. What a missed opportunity to preach the love of God to a captive heathen audience? In our zeal and self-righteousness, do we do the same to people who give us bad vibes thinking that we are exercising our gift of spiritual discernment? Are we not being carnal?

I once had a flat tire and stopped in front of a house. What a detestable house, I thought. What sort of people would want that in front of their house? The entire house was decorated with skeletons and witches' hats. I got out of the car, inspected the damage, and reached for my phone to ring for assistance from the Automobile Club. I was getting too old to lift the spare tyre from the back of the car. A cheerful voice interrupted, *"May I change your tyre? I am a mechanic by trade."* He came from the house which was so gruesomely decorated for Halloween. The couple had been sitting on the front veranda away from the heat caring for their little baby. He then proceeded to carefully unload everything I had in the boot (trunk) and changed the tyre. My mind scrambled in repentance what I should do. Fortunately, I had an unopened slab of Coca Cola cans which I handed to him as a way of thanks.

We could infer from the Bible that our actions can be justified because it warns us not to love the 'world' and not to associate with Christians who have walked away from God or bring their abominable lifestyles into the congregation. In terms of marriage, we are warned not to be unequally yoked and not to marry such, especially not a non-Christian. Charles and his former wife made a huge mistake when their daughter brought home a non-churched young man and they advised her to drop him and find a Christian boy at church. Sean eventually became the best Christian husband she could have ever asked her. But they struggled early in their marriage too. Nevertheless, the rule of thumb is that such marriages go 'pear shaped' when one of the partners decides to resume their worldly life.

Gloria and Charles thought that they had overcome cultural problems after about 4-5 months of marriage, but every now and then a niggling situation arises to demonstrate that one can't just wipe away a lifetime of habits and preferences overnight. Gloria has been a widow for eighteen years and had to stand on her own feet like a male fiercely fighting for existence against callous pastors in PNG who wished to evict their former Senior Pastor and her young children from the manse. She became a 'strong woman' intent on not marrying any of the many suitors that came her way until she found the right one. According to Gloria the right one came along after 18 years, until she was taken aback when she discovered my faults soon enough.

After another typical confrontation Gloria surprisingly came out with a statement that was already in my mind. She said words to the effect that if our marriage is prophetic of the perfection of the bride, and the merge between Messianic Jews and Christian Gentiles, then the process will be as painful as rubbing two sheets of sandpaper against each other. Nevertheless, the merge must and shall take place regardless of the rough road ahead. Jesus will settle for nothing less than perfection in his bride. We both agreed that we are surely in the Lord's will and that our rough edges have to be dealt with.

Repeated situations in our different idiosyncrasies distresses Gloria and arouses my anger. Gloria brought her fierce determination into our marriage and especially the fear that she will never really belong because of her colour, despite my reassurance that wherever we live together is her permanent home. What I offered her at the point of marriage parallels the offer of Christ,

"For as many as are led by the Spirit of God, they are the sons of God. For you have not received the spirit of bondage again to fear, but you have received the Spirit of adoption by which we cry, Abba, Father! The Spirit Himself bears witness with our spirit that we are the children of God. And if we are children, then we are heirs; heirs of God and joint-heirs with Christ; so that if we suffer with Him, we may also be glorified together. For I reckon that the sufferings of this present time are not worthy to be compared with the coming glory to be revealed in us." (Romans 8:14-18).

Insecurities can play havoc in the more vulnerable partner. Charles is easy going and befriends anyone, while Gloria tends to be aghast being driven by biblical principles and PNG culture to beware of potentially false friends, particularly females eying a white husband, wanting to destroy our marriage by witchcraft because of jealous rivalry.

The reader might be able to imagine the difficulty facing both Charles and Gloria when they come across people from PNG in public places. The eyes of these people light up having found a compatriot, and in the case of Charles, carrying a PNG-style shoulder bag (a bilum) which identifies him as being PNG-friendly. Some naturally want to start a conversation or become extremely friendly which arouses suspicions in Gloria who signals a clear message to me that I find extremely irritating. PNG and Caribbean women protect their 'white' husbands from enticing women by withdrawing from native company. Apparently, PNG men back home easily fall prey to scheming women, and vice-versa for PNG women.

For the sake of privacy, we shall not go into other matters, but are confident that every married couple can identify issues in one another's partners in marriage. So how does one cope with such things in life? Many, unfortunately, take unresolved issues with them to their graves. In Melbourne, Charles' church elders took a great deal of time visiting dear old people in nursing homes – except that they weren't so dear after all. The elders had a difficult time to bring up the unforgiveness they still harbour in their hearts – a sin that can lead to eternal death (*"Our Father, who art in heaven*, hallowed be your name, ..."*).

The Bible is clear on commendations such as *"do unto others as you wish they would do to you"*. Too often we meet grumpy people at church who have never brought into the open why they might detest the other. How did Jesus respond in such situations? Even at his betrayal in the Garden of Gethsemane Jesus called Judas 'friend' knowing full well what the purpose of the kiss was.

Above all the spiritual gifts, the apostle Paul highlighted love as the greatest of all in Galatians 5:14, *"For the law is fulfilled in one word even in this: You shall love your neighbour as yourself"*. Need we quote more scriptures from the apostles or from Yeshua himself?

The next question, of course is, how are we to love our neighbour in keeping with all the scriptures on love in the Bible? We need to apply common sense in every individual situation. Firstly forgiveness, and secondly to assess the circumstances and despite our reluctance, on how we can love the unlovable or those who have deliberately stabbed us in the back. In extreme cases, the scripture gives us sound advice. We need to apply this principle albeit watered down in most situations.

One published example in his own biography might serve as an example how to respond to years of bitter differences. Kevin Connor, one of Australia's outstanding Bible teachers, whose many books are  distributed by the Word and Koorong Bookstores, heard accusations of immorality against the two most two senior leaders of the church, an apostle and a prophet (*This is My Story – With Lessons Along the Way*, KJC Publications C, Australia, 2008).

He brought up what he believed at an elder's meeting one night supported with testimonies by others. The persons named violently rejected the accusations and were strongly defended by the rest of the eldership. Kevin was ordered to repent, together with his wife, and were harassed over many months until they nearly had nervous breakdowns. They eventually moved to Portland, Oregon USA, where they continued teaching Bible School. Lo and behold, about ten years later the accusations he had brought to the leadership meeting proved themselves true. The eldership virtually ran to him begging them to come back to resume their old duties. Kevin's response was brief and appropriate, *"We have forgiven you, but we certainly won't be joining you"* – words to that effect.

Can you identify the love of God in the following example from the Bible? *"Your own members are aware that there is sexual sin going on among them. This kind of sin is not even heard of among unbelievers—a man is actually married to his father's wife. You're being arrogant when you should have been more upset about this. If you had been upset, the man who did this would have been removed from among you. Although I'm not physically present with you, I am with you in spirit. I have already judged the man who did this as though I were present with you. When you have gathered together, I am with you in spirit. Then, in the name of our Lord Jesus, and with his power, hand such a person over to Satan to destroy his corrupt nature so that his spiritual nature may be saved on the day of the Lord. It's not good for you to brag. Don't you know that a little yeast spreads through the whole batch of dough? Remove the old yeast (of sin) so that you may be a new batch of dough, since you don't actually have the yeast (of sin) Christ, our Passover lamb, has been sacrificed. So we must not celebrate our festival with the old yeast (of sin) or with the yeast of vice and wickedness. Instead, we must celebrate it with the bread of purity and truth that has no yeast. In my letter to you I told you not to associate with people who continue to commit sexual sins. I didn't tell you that you could not have any contact with unbelievers who commit sexual sins, are greedy, are dishonest, or worship false gods. If that were the case, you would have to leave this world. Now, what I meant was that you should not associate with people who call themselves brothers or sisters in the Christian faith but live in sexual sin, are greedy, worship false gods, use abusive language, get drunk, or are dishonest. Don't eat with such people. After all, do I have any business judging those who are outside (the Christian faith)? Isn't it your business to judge those who are inside? God will judge those who are outside. Remove that wicked man from among you,"* (1 Corinthians 5:1-13, GW).

Depending on the situation, we may water this principle down a little on lesser matters. Being unpleasant to outsiders or immediately rejecting them if they approach one in a friendly manner, even if they bear a spirit not of Christ, is surely not what the gospel of Jesus Christ is all about. In that case we have sorely missed out on an opportunity to demonstrate the love of God. In fact, we will have turned them away from Christ. The Lord will surely be greatly displeased. Who knows what our encounter or friendly conversation might lead to? Everybody wants to be loved, even the unlovely are sulking most probably because they have never experienced love (1 Peter Chapter 3).

"How horrible it will be for you when everyone says nice things about you. That's the way their ancestors treated the false prophets. "But I tell everyone who is listening: Love your enemies. Be kind to those who hate you. Bless those who curse you. Pray for those who insult you. If someone strikes you on the cheek, offer the other cheek as well. If someone takes your coat, don't stop him from taking your shirt. Give to everyone who asks you for something. If

someone takes what is yours, don't insist on getting it back. "Do for other people everything you want them to do for you. "If you love those who love you, do you deserve any thanks for that? Even sinners love those who love them. If you help those who help you, do you deserve any thanks for that? Sinners do that too. If you lend anything to those from whom you expect to get something back, do you deserve any thanks for that? Sinners also lend to sinners to get back what they lend. Rather, love your enemies, help them, and lend to them without expecting to get anything back. Then you will have a great reward. You will be the children of the Most High God. After all, he is kind to unthankful and evil people" (Luke 6:26-35).

Question 1

In several instances Jesus referred to those who thought they had done the will of God, "Depart from me for I never knew you".

- Using a Bible Concordance or Bible software find those instances in Scripture.
- Who was he addressing? Christians (Messianic or otherwise) or non-Christians?
- How is it possible to denounce those who have led others to Christ and demonstrated gifts and miracles and prophesied for the good of others?

Question 2

English is not a particularly rich language. The Greeks had three words for love.

- Find out using a dictionary or Dr Google what they are.
- What is the difference between them?
- Which are the carnal and the spiritual forms of love?
- If we only practice the highest spiritual form of love, can we truly love our neighbour in accordance with God's commands?
- If not, why not?

Question 3

Think of lovely people in your community. Then answer the following:

- Is it necessary to be a Christian to be thought of as a good person?
- List why you think they are lovely people. What do they do to make you think them lovely? What signs would you be looking for to find out whether they are Christians or not?

Question 4

Think about the following true scenario Charles heard. An old gentleman was sharing his life's experiences in a home fellowship of our church one night. He said that when he was a younger man in the workforce, he fell into the habit of having his homemade lunch on a park bench daily with the same fellow worker over a period of 25 years. They discussed their families and, above all, their love of football and the game they were looking forward to each week. Who was injured and how would that effect the game? After about 25 years one of them made a side remark which immediately prompted a question by the other, "*Are you by any chance a Christian*"?

- How do you think this true account ended?
- What is your assessment of the relationship between the two gentlemen?
- Had they been obedient to the command of the resurrected Christ (Matthew 18:18-20)?
- What about you? Are you willing to witness your faith to others in your daily life?

The Word is as a Fire

Our hope is that the reader will not shirk from the occasional challenge presented by Gloria and myself. They have been given in love so that you may reap more in heaven than what you might be anticipating right now. Most Christians aim for too little. We cannot help but present the Word of God as we see it. All of us need to grow closer to Christ. It's good to keep in mind what the apostle Paul said in Romans 11:1, "*So take a look at the goodness and the severity of God; severity to those who have fallen, but goodness to you, on condition that you continue to live by His goodness; otherwise, you too will be pruned away*" (Romans 11:22, Williams). Many Christians don't take the word 'severity' seriously enough.

The Word of the Lord is as a consuming Fire

The Lord *Esh Oklah* and the Holy Spirit *Ruach HaKodesh* is a consuming fire that destroys all wickedness in men and in the heavens (Deuteronomy 4:23-25, 9:3; Matthew 3:11; Hebrews 10:31, 12:29; 2 Thessalonians 2:8).

"Look! The Lord is coming from far away, burning with anger, surrounded by thick, rising smoke. His lips are filled with fury; his words consume like fire" (Isaiah 30:27, NLT).

"For the word of God is alive and active. Sharper than any double-edged sword, it penetrates even to dividing soul and spirit, joints and marrow; it judges the thoughts and attitudes of the heart" (Hebrews 4:12, NIV).

Acknowledgement of images

David Ben-Gurion proclaiming Israeli independence from the United Kingdom on 14 May 1948, below a portrait of Theodor Herzl. By Rudi Weissenstein: Public Domain
https://commons.wikimedia.org/w/index.php?curid=1247313

Law of return. By user: NYC2TLV
Public Domain
https://commons.wikimedia.org/w/index.php?curid=13734465

Close up of a Mezuzah. By Joseph Sherman:
Public Doman
wikimedia.org/wikipedia/commons/1/1f/ShinMezuzahJosephSherman.jpg

Gulf of Aqaba. By Odie5533:
Public Domain
https://commons.wikimedia.org/w/index.php?curid=6903961

Samson. Gustave Doré - Doré's English Bible 1866:
Public Domain
https://en.wikipedia.org/wiki/Samson#/media/File:064.The_Death_of_Samson.jpg

Other Books by Charles Pallaghy

The Bible and Science, 1984. Jeff Hammond and Charles Pallaghy, Acacia Press, Blackburn, Australia

Alkitab dan Ilmu Pengetahuan, 1984. Jeff Hammond and Charles Pallaghy, Jakarta, Indonesia

End Times: According to Scripture, 2023 update. Charles Pallaghy, Bookside Press, Toronto, Canada (in colour, high resolution and A4 format)

Immortal to the End: A Challenging True Story of the Supernatural, 2024. Charles Pallaghy, Bookside Press, Toronto, Canada (In press).

9 781778 833656